CHRISTIAN HEROES: THEN & NOW

ERIC LIDDELL

Something Greater Than Gold

CHRISTIAN HEROES: THEN & NOW

ERIC LIDDELL

Something Greater Than Gold

JANET & GEOFF BENGE

YWAM Publishing is the publishing ministry of Youth With A Mission. Youth With A Mission (YWAM) is an international missionary organization of Christians from many denominations dedicated to presenting Jesus Christ to this generation. To this end, YWAM has focused its efforts in three main areas: (1) training and equipping believers for their part in fulfilling the Great Commission (Matthew 28:19), (2) personal evangelism, and (3) mercy ministry (medical and relief work).

For a free catalog of books and materials, contact:

YWAM Publishing
P.O. Box 55787, Seattle, WA 98155
(425) 771-1153 or (800) 922-2143
www.ywampublishing.com

Library of Congress Cataloging-in-Publication Data

Benge, Janet, 1958–
Eric Liddell: something greater than gold / by Janet and Geoff Benge.
p. cm. — (Christian heroes, then & now)
Includes bibliographical references.
Summary: A biography of the Scottish missionary and runner who won a gold medal in the 1924 Olympics and went on to do missionary work in China.
ISBN 1-57658-137-3
1. Liddell, Eric, 1902–1945—Juvenile literature.
2. Missionaries—China—Biography—Juvenile literature.
3. Missionaries—Scotland—Biography—Juvenile literature.
4. Runners (Sports)—Scotland—Biography—Juvenile literature.
[1. Liddell, Eric, 1902–1945. 2. Missionaries. 3. Runners (Sports)]
I. Benge, Geoff, 1954– . II. Title. III. Series.
BV3427.L52B46 1998
266'.52'092—dc21
[b] 98-30892
CIP
AC

Eric Liddell: Something Greater Than Gold

ISBN 978-1-57658-137-7 (paperback)
ISBN 978-1-57658-573-3 (e-book)

Fifteenth printing 2024

Published by YWAM Publishing
P.O. Box 55787
Seattle, WA 98155

Printed in the United States of America.

Christian Heroes: Then & Now

Adoniram Judson
Albert Schweitzer
Amy Carmichael
Betty Greene
Brother Andrew
Cameron Townsend
Charles Mulli
Clarence Jones
Corrie ten Boom
Count Zinzendorf
C. S. Lewis
C. T. Studd
David Bussau
David Livingstone
Dietrich Bonhoeffer
D. L. Moody
Elisabeth Elliot
Eric Liddell
Florence Young
Francis Asbury
George Müller
Gladys Aylward
Helen Roseveare
Hudson Taylor
Ida Scudder
Isobel Kuhn
Jacob DeShazer
Jim Elliot
John Flynn
John Newton
John Wesley
John Williams
Jonathan Goforth
Klaus-Dieter John
Lillian Trasher
Loren Cunningham
Lottie Moon
Mary Slessor
Mildred Cable
Nate Saint
Norman Grubb
Paul Brand
Rachel Saint
Richard Wurmbrand
Rowland Bingham
Samuel Zwemer
Sundar Singh
Wilfred Grenfell
William Booth
William Carey

Available in paperback, e-book, and audiobook formats.Unit study curriculum guides are available for select biographies.

www.YWAMpublishing.com

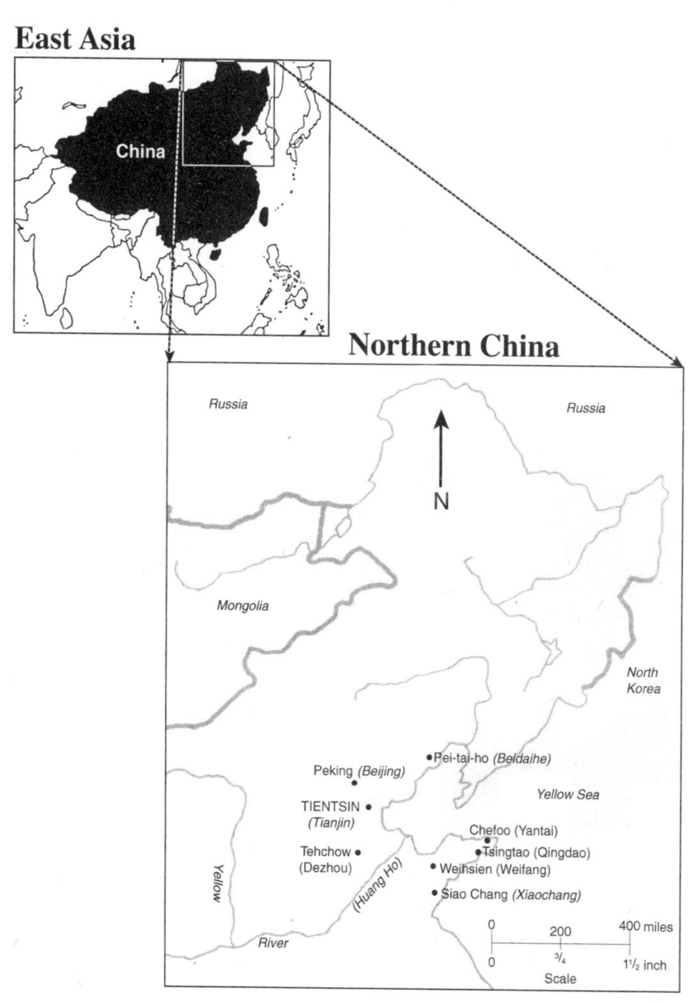
East Asia
China
Northern China
Russia
Russia
N
Mongolia
North Korea
Pei-tai-ho (Beidaihe)
Peking (Beijing)
Yellow Sea
TIENTSIN (Tianjin)
Chefoo (Yantai)
Tsingtao (Qingdao)
Tehchow (Dezhou)
Weihsien (Weifang)
Siao Chang (Xiaochang)
Yellow
(Huang Ho)
River
0 200 400 miles
0 3/4 1 1/2 inch
Scale

Contents

Chapter 1

Doing the Impossible

Crack! The sound of the starter's pistol echoed around Colombes Stadium. The final of the 400 meters had begun. Eric Liddell lunged forward. The spikes on his black leather running shoes gripped the rolled cinder surface of the track. Puffs of gray cinders burst from under his shoes with each stride. Eric was running in the outside lane, the worst to be in. Running next to him was the American, Horatio Fitch, the favorite to win the gold medal. Fitch had set a new world record for the distance in his heat to qualify for the final. Running next to Fitch was Joseph Imbach, the Swiss runner who had also broken the world record in his qualifying heat. Everyone expected the battle for the gold medal to be between these two men. The cheers of the crowd rose in anticipation.

As the field of runners streaked down the back straightaway from the starting line, though, it was Eric Liddell in the lead. As the runners rounded the corner and passed the 200-meter mark, the midway point of the race, Eric had run the first half of the race in the amazingly fast time of 22.2 seconds.

Eric could hear the feet of the other runners stomping against the cinder track as the men strained to catch up to him. The crowd could see that Guy Butler, the other British runner in the race, was three meters behind Eric. Horatio Fitch was also gaining fast, but with no time to look back, Eric threw all his effort into running.

As the crowd realized that Eric Liddell was not falling back into third or fourth place as expected, it became strangely silent, too stunned to cheer. Those who knew anything about running techniques just shook their heads. A runner couldn't sprint for the whole 400 meters of the race. To them it was obvious: Eric Liddell was a 100-meter runner who had no idea how to run a 400-meter race. A runner who sprints from the start in such a race, as though he's running in a 100-meter dash, will use up all his energy and have no stamina for a final burst of speed at the end of the race. The crowd waited silently for Eric to fade.

By the time Eric had rounded the bend, Horatio Fitch had closed to within two meters of taking the lead. Eric could sense his presence. Believing that Fitch was making his move on Eric, the crowd burst to life again.

Just as everyone thought that Horatio Fitch was about to pass Eric, a gasp went through the crowd. It couldn't be. It was impossible. No one had ever run the 400 meters like this before. But it was true. Just when the crowd was sure that he was fading, Eric threw back his head and flung his arms about like a drowning man. With that, he mustered a burst of speed and pulled away from Horatio Fitch. Instead of slowing down, Eric was running the second half of the race faster than the first. Sensing an upset, the crowd erupted into cheers for Eric. Many frantically waved him on with Union Jacks.

As he reached the end of the home straight, Eric threw himself forward across the finish line five meters ahead of Horatio Fitch! He took several more steps to slow down and then collapsed into the arms of the British coach. Eric sucked air into his lungs as fast and as hard as he could as he lay on his back on the track.

Thundering applause erupted throughout the stadium. The noise was deafening. It was reported later that it could be heard all over Paris. Eric Liddell had done the impossible, and the crowd had watched him do it. Now the people wanted to raise their voices and celebrate the win with him.

Finally, after several minutes, the noised died down enough to hear the official announcement that Eric not only had won the race but also had set a new world record. Eric Liddell had broken the old record by two-tenths of a second. The crowd went wild again.

Some of the members of the British Olympic team made their way onto the field and hoisted Eric onto their shoulders. They carried him along the track until they were in front of the official box where the Prince of Wales, the future King of England, stood cheering. The prince acknowledged Eric, who in turn bowed his head to him as a mark of respect.

All around Eric, people were cheering, waving Union Jacks, shaking Eric's hand, and patting the runner on the back. Emotions surged inside Eric's exhausted body. Eric felt proud and happy all at once. He smiled to himself in satisfaction and marveled at how different the scene was from anything he'd ever dreamed of as a small boy growing up on the coastal plain of northern China.

Chapter 2

Going Home

Four-year-old Eric Liddell had a wonderful life. He lived at a large London Missionary Society compound in Siao Chang on the Great Plain of North China. Eric, along with his six-year-old brother Robert and Jenny, his three-year-old sister, had free run of the place. There were four large houses inside the compound walls, plus two schools, one for boys and one for girls, and a church. Eric's father, James Liddell, preached in the church, and his mother, Mary, helped teach school. As a nurse, Eric's mother also took care of many of the local children when they were sick.

Sometimes visitors to the Siao Chang compound thought little Eric was a Chinese boy. Eric dressed in a blue padded jacket and pants like the rest of the village children, and he chatted away to his friends in perfect Chinese. But when he took his cap off, it was obvious he wasn't Chinese. Despite his local dress, he had straight blond hair and big blue eyes. "The laddie has fair Scottish coloring," his mother would tell visitors as she patted Eric on the head and sent him back outside to play with his friends or his pet goat.

Eric often heard his parents talk about the hills of "bonnie Scotland," and he tried to imagine what the country would be like. His mother said it never got too cold or too hot in Scotland, unlike China, where it fell below freezing in winter and soared to 110 degrees Fahrenheit in summer. She also told Eric of huge areas there, as far as a person could see, with not a house or farm in sight. Eric found this hard to believe, especially when he clambered up on top of the six-foot-high mud wall that surrounded the mission compound. The Great Plain of North China surrounded Siao Chang, and across the plain lived ten million people in ten thousand villages dotted close together. Stretched between the villages was an almost endless patchwork of wheat and millet fields divided by snaking muddy streams and waterways that had been used for centuries to irrigate the land. Eric couldn't look anywhere around this landscape and not see people, houses, and farms. It was the only landscape he had known in his young life, and it was very hard for him to imagine anything else.

Eric's parents had come to China before Eric was born. James Liddell arrived in China as a missionary in 1898, and soon afterwards, his fiance, Mary, joined him there. The two were married in Shanghai in 1899 and then sent by the London Missionary Society (LMS) to work in Mongolia. Soon after arriving in Mongolia, though, a terrible rebellion broke out in China. A group of men calling themselves the "League of Righteous and Harmonious Fists," or "Boxers" for short, stirred up hatred among the Chinese people toward all foreigners.

The Boxers believed that they possessed magical powers. They thought that their bodies could stop bullets and cannonballs and that they could ward off sword blows with their bare arms. Many of the uneducated peasants in China believed the Boxers and were terrified of them.

The Boxer Rebellion erupted in June 1900. Chinese people were encouraged to rise up and kill all the foreigners who had humiliated their country for so long. The Boxers especially wanted foreign missionaries killed because they were bringing another religion to the people of China. Many people did join with the Boxers and killed missionaries, along with many Chinese Christians. The Boxer Rebellion started when the German ambassador to Peking was assassinated. By the time it was finally put down by a combined force of twenty thousand foreign troops, two hundred missionaries, including women and children, and over thirty thousand Chinese Christians had been killed.

Mongolia was one of the first places the Boxers attacked. James Liddell had fled the mission station there with Mary, who was expecting their first child. The couple had left all their belongings behind except for a small suitcase of clothes. In fear for their lives at every turn, they made the long and tortuous journey south several hundred miles to Shanghai. There they waited at the LMS compound before moving on to Tientsin. While waiting for the rebellion to die down, James Liddell traveled back to Mongolia to see what had become of the mission and the Chinese Christians he had been forced to leave behind. He found the mission station destroyed and the local Christians in hiding. The area still wasn't safe for missionaries to return to.

When James Liddell reported his findings to the London Missionary Society, the society sent the Liddells to one of its established mission centers in Siao Chang, a small village in the central area of the Great Plain. By then, the couple had two sons. On January 16, 1902, eighteen months after the birth of her first son, Robert, Mary Liddell had given birth to a blond-haired, blue-eyed, dimple-chinned baby boy. The baby had been named Eric Henry Liddell. The baby was to have been called Henry Eric Liddell until a missionary friend pointed out that the initials spelled "H. E. L." James Liddell quickly switched his new son's first names around.

Even though the Boxer Rebellion had been put down, in many parts of China, feelings of hatred and anger towards foreigners still simmered below the surface. This was not the case in Siao Chang, however. The Chinese Christians who lived there were eager to welcome missionaries back. When Eric's parents arrived at the compound for the first time, a banner was hanging over the village gate. It read "Chung Wai I Chai," which James and Mary Liddell knew meant "Chinese and foreigners, all one home." How glad the Liddells were to finally be somewhere safe.

After James and Mary Liddell had been in China for nine years, the London Missionary Society decided the family should return to Scotland for a year's break, or furlough, as it was officially called.

"We're going home," Robert yelled as he raced out the door into the courtyard where Eric and Jenny were playing with a new batch of kittens.

"Home?" questioned five-year-old Eric. "We are home."

"No, our other home, silly, to Scotland," replied his older and wiser brother, who had never actually been there.

That afternoon, the Liddell family began to pack and prepare for their trip home. Several days later, the family made their way from Siao Chang to Tientsin, where they caught a boat to Shanghai. Eric had been with his family to the beach before, but he had never been on a boat. He stood in amazement and peered over the side until Tientsin disappeared completely from view. In Shanghai, they boarded a German steamer for the six-week voyage from Shanghai to Southampton. After arriving in England, the family caught a train to London, where James and Mary Liddell met with the leaders of the London Missionary Society and gave them a detailed report of their work. Then they climbed aboard another train for the final leg of the trip home to Scotland.

As the train rolled into Scotland, Eric's eyes grew big as he looked out the window. There was so much empty land. Sheep grazed among castle ruins, and the wide green valleys were dotted with small stone cottages. Everything delighted Eric; Scotland was so different from China, and so different from anything he had imagined. Finally, the train drew to a stop at the village of Dryman on the shores of Loch Lomond. James Liddell announced to his young son that they were finally "home."

Eric loved Dryman. His parents rented a house there, and he was able to explore the same places his father had explored as a child. Eric's grandfather owned a small grocery store in Dryman. It didn't take Eric long to figure out that he liked the aniseed balls, licorice allsorts, and English toffees sold in the store. Grandfather Liddell also ran a side business transporting people and packages to and from the railway station. The village and the station were about a mile apart. Many times Eric would perch on top of the horse-drawn wagon with his grandfather, looking importantly down on the world as they rode to the station to meet the train.

The yearlong furlough in Dryman sped by, and at the end of it, Eric's mother had something important to tell her sons. The two boys would not be returning to China with the rest of the family. It was time for them to start their formal education in a proper English school. In 1908, it was normal for the children of missionaries to attend boarding schools in England while their parents served overseas in foreign countries.

Six-year-old Eric clung to his brother as the two boys followed their mother up the steps and into the dreary stone administration building of London's School for the Sons of Missionaries. (In 1912, while Eric and Robert were still enrolled there, the school changed its name to Eltham College.) The school had been started in 1842 by the London Missionary Society, and all of the one hundred fifty boys who attended it were sons of missionaries, just as the sign on the gate said. All going well, Robert and Eric would attend the school until they graduated and were ready for university.

An hour after arriving, the boys had been outfitted with gray flannel shorts, jacket, tie, and cap, just like all the other students. Then they were shown to their beds at the end of a long row of narrow cots that ran the length of the upstairs dorm room. Beside each cot was a washstand that held a basin and water jug. The brothers were told to hang their things on the hook beside their cots and join the rest of the class for a cricket lesson on the back field. Mary Liddell slipped quietly away from the school while her boys were being introduced to the meaning of a wicket, a maiden over, and other details of cricket. It would be seven years before Eric and

Robert would see their mother again, and thirteen years before they saw their father.

After his carefree life in China and the wilds of the Scottish highlands, Eric found it difficult to adjust to living in the gray stone building in London. He missed his parents, his younger sister Jenny, and the goats and the kittens he'd had in China. Since he was small for his age and very shy, Eric let Robert do the talking for them both. He would freeze with terror if someone asked him a question when Robert wasn't around.

At school, every part of Eric and Robert's life, along with the lives of the other students, was organized by someone else. The students sat in long rows when eating their meals, with a schoolmaster looking on to make sure they used proper manners. The Liddell brothers missed Chinese food a lot. They were not used to eating the bread and dripping and bowl of gray oatmeal they were served each morning for breakfast. Eric longed for a bowl of soya beans or millet.

All of the boys in school marched into class in rows and sat without talking as their teacher read the day's lessons. After school they all went to the study hall, where they did their homework, once again sitting in rows. Each Thursday evening they wrote letters to their parents under the supervision of one of the schoolmasters. All this work was hard for a young boy not used to attending school.

As with most schools in the early 1900s, the hours of hard study went hand in hand with a lot of vigorous exercise. Sports were not something extra a boy might do for a hobby; they were a serious part of the school day. All the boys learned to play rugby in winter. In summer they played cricket and competed in many track and field events.

This emphasis on sports was meant to teach British boys how to play by rules, how to respect authority, and how to be part of a team. While Eric didn't find much joy in class work, he enjoyed sports. In one of his letters to the family in China, ten-year-old Eric wrote, "I don't think much of lessons, but I can run."

And so he could! Both Eric and Robert excelled at every sport they tried.

Another activity all the students were expected to be a part of was the school play. The drama teacher took great pride in presenting a play each year, and there was a lot of competition for the leading roles. Even the girls' parts were all played by the boys. One year it was decided that the play would be *Alice In Wonderland.* Eric didn't want a leading role; in fact, he didn't want a role at all. It was agony for him to think of getting up in front of so many people. As it turned out, the drama teacher cast him as the dormouse, a shy little creature with hardly a word to say. The part was just right for Eric, who did a wonderful job. Eric didn't even have to pretend to be shy! After the play and until the time he left Eltham College at nineteen, his nickname was "The Mouse."

For summer holidays, the two boys would take the train to Dryman to stay with their grandfather.

On shorter holidays, they either stayed at school or stayed with some of their friends.

Eric would have liked to have been more involved in things at school, but he was just too shy. Once there was a tennis match against a nearby girls' school, but Eric pulled out at the last minute. He couldn't imagine what he would say to a girl when he got to her school. There were also Bible studies the boys could attend if they chose. Eric liked to go along, but he always sat near the back so that he could make a quick exit if he were called upon to answer a question or make a comment.

The years at school rolled by, with each new year not much different from the one before. That is, until 1914, when Eric was twelve years old. Two events happened that Eric would remember for the rest of his life. The first event was a happy one. Eric's mother gave birth to another baby boy, Ernest. Eric was eager to see his new little brother, and his mother promised to bring Ernest and Jenny to London for a few weeks' visit in 1915. The second event was a terrible and frightening one. A great war, which would eventually be known as the First World War, started in Europe. Germany and the Austro-Hungarian Empire were on one side, with France, Great Britain, and Russia on the other. Many of the senior boys at the school volunteered to fight for the British. Before they left for the battlefield, they proudly visited Eltham College in their new khaki uniforms, and each boy carried a modern short-magazine Lee Enfield rifle.

Within weeks, many of these new recruits had been killed on the battlefields of Flanders, in France. Like the rest of the boys at school, Eric came to dread the daily assembly where the latest list of dead and injured "old boys" was read. It was not easy to listen to the names being read. These dead and wounded soldiers were not just names, they were people—friends the boys had played cricket and rugby with, friends who had helped the younger boys in study hall. It was like losing one big brother after another, and it went on for four years.

Sports though, seemed to cheer Eric up. Like his older brother, Eric showed a lot of promise. By the time Robert had reached his senior year at Eltham College, Eric was his only real competition in sports. By 1918, when Eric was sixteen and Robert was eighteen, the brothers were the two athletic stars of the school. The 1918 sports page in the school record book read as follows:

First in Cross Country, High Jump, and Hurdling, Robert Liddell.

First in Long Jump, 100-Yard Dash, and Quarter-Mile Race, Eric Liddell.

Where the one brother came in first, the other was always in second place! Not only that, Eric and Robert both played rugby for the First Fifteen and cricket for the First Eleven (the school's top teams in each sport). Robert, and then Eric, was also made captain of most of the school's sports teams.

In 1918, just as Robert was old enough to consider signing up to fight, the First World War ended.

That year, instead of going off to war, Robert left Eltham College for Edinburgh University to study to become a doctor. Edinburgh was located on the east coast of Scotland. For the first time in his life, Eric was alone, away from every member of his family. But he had little time to be lonely. He had to study for some difficult and important exams coming up at the end of the 1919 school year. And, as usual, involvement in sports also kept him busy. Eric did well in both pursuits. He passed his exams and set a new school record of 10.2 seconds for the 100-yard sprint, a school record that to this day has not been broken.

A year later, Eric left Eltham College and rode the train north to Edinburgh University. It was a very exciting time for him. His mother was coming home to Scotland, along with seventeen-year-old Jenny and six-year-old Ernest. They would all live together again in Edinburgh, and Eric's father would join them there a year later. Finally, the whole family would be together again.

Sure enough, in 1921 James Liddell returned to Scotland. Eric was six years old when he had last seen his father. After the two of them had caught up on each other's lives, James Liddell asked his son what he wanted to do once he finished studying for his degree in math and science. Eric had to confess that he wasn't too sure. Never in his wildest dreams, though, could he have imagined that before he even graduated he would be the most famous man in Scotland.

Chapter 3

A Rising Sports Star

Eric loved attending university. He was free to come and go as he pleased, and at the end of each day, he had a home-cooked meal waiting for him to eat with his family. He kept busy with classwork and got good grades, especially in chemistry and mathematics. When he wanted a break from studying, he would get together with a group of friends and play a friendly game of rugby or throw a cricket ball around for an hour or two. It wasn't long before these friends began to notice that Eric was a very fast runner. One friend, Bill Harvey, who had done some running himself, invited Eric to participate in the University Athletic Sports competition. At first Eric refused; he was at university to get an education, not to spend his time running around a track. But Bill Harvey wanted someone to practice his coaching skills on, and in the end he managed to persuade Eric to enter the 100-yard and 220-yard races.

Even though he had agreed to participate in the competition, Eric had no intention of letting running interfere with his other activities. He and four other students had made plans to take a six-day bike ride from Edinburgh to Ben Nevis and back during their Easter break. Ben Nevis was Scotland's highest mountain, and Eric wanted to climb it and see the view from the top. But Bill Harvey didn't want him to go on the trip. It was only six weeks until the competition, and he had read that bike riding stretched the wrong muscles for running. Eric didn't believe him, and he cycled off. A week later, upon returning from the trip, Eric discovered that Bill Harvey had been right. When he tried to run, his leg muscles stiffened up, and he knew it was going to be a tough job to get back in shape for the race.

The five weeks leading up to the competition were busy. Bill Harvey took coaching seriously and spent many hours with Eric, massaging his leg muscles to make them stretch the right way again. As race day approached, Eric began to get nervous. It was one thing to run at Eltham College, where everyone knew him and where his own brother was the main competition. It was another thing to run in front of a thousand strangers!

Finally, in May 1921, the day of the competition rolled around. Bill Harvey had worked hard to get Eric's body in shape for his first competition in Scotland. Of course, Eric didn't think he could win his races. Scotland's best running star, Innes Stewart, was competing against him in both events. Eric did hope, however, to be among the first three runners to finish the race. Eric Liddell and Innes Stewart were set to race against each other in the first heat of the 100-yard sprint.

Eric jogged nervously to the starting line. It was a hot day, and he wiped his brow on his white singlet before crouching at the starting line beside the other runners in the heat. The starter's pistol let out a loud crack, and the runners sprang forward. The crowd cheered wildly for Innes Stewart, and in less than eleven seconds it was over. As expected, Innes Stewart had finished first, but right on his heels was Eric Liddell.

The final of the race was held later that afternoon. The race played out much as the heat had in the morning, but with just one difference. This time, it was Eric Liddell who burst through the finish tape to win the race and Innes Stewart who was close behind. Eric had won the 100-yard dash. The crowd roared its approval.

The next day it was time for the 220-yard dash, Innes Stewart's specialty race. Innes was sure that no one in Scotland could beat him, and he was right. Eric came in second, losing by exactly one inch! The crowd went wild with excitement, as though it knew it was seeing not one but two of Scotland's greatest future athletes. Eric stood proudly on the podium as he received his prize. He was thrilled to have a first and a second place in the two races. As the crowd clapped and cheered, it didn't know it then, but it had just seen something no one else would ever see on Scottish soil again: Eric Liddell coming in second in a race. From that time on, Eric won every single race he ever entered in Scotland.

Eric expected everything to return to normal after his win. Things always had after he'd won a race at Eltham College. However, as he soon found out, things were a little different at university. As of May 1921, Eric Liddell was the top 100-yard sprinter and the second fastest 220-yard runner in the whole university. This meant that he was Edinburgh University's best hope for a medal at the Scottish University Sports Competition in two months. As such, he had a duty to run for his university. While he worried about his studies suffering, Eric knew he had no choice; he had to compete. Besides, he was enjoying running.

The University Athletics Club decided that Bill Harvey wasn't experienced enough as a coach for its top runner. Bill was replaced by Tom McKerchar, a good coach with a lot of experience. Tom McKerchar took Eric to Powderhill Stadium, where he trained several other top Scottish athletes. The first time Eric walked into the stadium, he nearly walked right back out again. A group of experienced runners were training, and they looked completely silly to Eric. To warm up, they were running in place on tiptoe, like oversized ballerinas, waving their arms wildly and rolling their shoulders at the same time. Eric told himself there was no way he was ever going to do that in front of a crowd.

Tom McKerchar had agreed to coach Eric because of his win at the university competition, but as he studied Eric's terrible running style more closely, he wondered how Eric had managed to win at all. Eric had been told many times that his running style was odd. He would fling his head back and pull his arms forward almost as if he were boxing at some invisible target. He lost count of how many times Tom McKerchar tried to make him run looking straight ahead with his arms gliding smoothly at his sides. But no matter how hard he tried, Eric simply couldn't change. However, Tom McKerchar did succeed in getting Eric to do the "ballerina warm-up," and before long, Eric was prancing around on tiptoe before a race, like everyone else.

The Scottish University Sports Competition quickly rolled around. Tom McKerchar was pleased with Eric's speed, if not his style. Eric won the 100-yard sprint, with Innes Stewart coming in second. Their one-two finishes helped Edinburgh University earn the proud honor of having the best athletics team in Scotland.

In two track and field competitions, Eric Liddell had proved himself to be a top athlete, and the more he ran, the more he won. Time after time he broke records. He ran the 100-yard dash in 10.2 seconds and the 220 in 21.8 seconds, a full two-tenths of a second better than the previous record. He also ran the 440-yard (quarter-mile) race in 52.6 seconds, so much faster than it had ever been run before at the Scottish Inter-University Games that it took another thirty-five years before anyone bettered it.

Before long, Eric had a group of supporters who traveled from place to place to watch him run. He found this embarrassing at first, but he also thought it was a nice gesture for so many people to give up their free time to come and encourage him.

As impressed as these supporters were with Eric's speed, they were more impressed with his attitude. Although he wanted to win each race and trained hard to do so, he always had a good attitude towards the other competitors. Before a race he would shake each contestant's hand and wish him success. He never said "good luck," because he didn't believe luck had much to do with winning a race. For him, it was skill and training that won races.

Other gestures also showed his good sportsmanship. Back then, at the beginning of a race, a runner would dig himself two small holes in the turf or cinder track just behind the starting line. Into these holes, the runner would place his toes to push off and get a better start. Eric used a small steel trowel for this purpose, and when he'd finished digging his holes, he would always offer the trowel to the other runners to use. On one occasion, another runner from Edinburgh University had drawn the outside lane in the 440-yard race. The 440-yard race was one lap around the track, and runners hated to be in the outside lane for it. There were few markings on the track, and the person running in the outside lane was likely to get bumped around. So Eric quietly swapped lanes with the other runner. The change in lane made no difference to him; he still won.

With each victory came a prize, and soon the Liddell family was facing a problem it had never encountered before: keeping valuable items in the house. It didn't take long before the Liddells' house on Gillespie Crescent in Edinburgh was brimming with Eric's prizes and trophies. There were the usual gold and silver cups and bowls, along with cake stands, clocks, leather suitcases, vases, enough watches for everyone in the family to have three apiece, cases of cutlery, pens, salad bowls, and silver tea sets. With so much gold and silver in the house, Eric's mother worried that the house would be burglarized. She hid many of the most valuable prizes under her bed each night. But the house was never broken into, and Eric just kept collecting prizes each time he ran.

Running wasn't the only thing Eric excelled at. Because of his speed, he won a place on the Edinburgh University rugby team. From his earliest days at Eltham College, he'd enjoyed playing rugby. His position was on the wing. A rugby team consists of fifteen players, eight forwards and seven backs. After the ball is freed from a ruck or scrum by the eight forwards using their feet, it is picked up by the halfback and passed along the line of backs. At the end of the back line are the wings, one on the left side of the field and one on the right. When the wing finally receives the ball, it is his job to try to get himself and the ball as far up the field towards the goal line as possible. All the while, the opposing team is looking to tackle whoever has the ball. With his speed, the position on the wing was tailor-made for Eric. When he got the ball, he seemed able to make incredible plays and gain valuable field position for his side.

In his second year at Edinburgh, the university rugby team toured England, winning six of its seven games. Because of Eric's outstanding play in these games, the selectors for the Scottish national rugby team named Eric to their side.

Rugby was and still is a matter of great national pride to the people of the British Isles. Fierce competition exists between the Scottish, Welsh, Irish, and English teams. In 1922, Scotland played Wales at Arms Park in Cardiff, Wales. The Scots had not won a match against the Welsh since 1890! Eric and the other Scottish wing, Leslie Gracie, were the stars of the game. They played a masterful game of rugby, and when the final whistle sounded, Scotland had beaten Wales eleven points to eight. Amazingly, when the game was over, the losing Welsh team scooped Eric Liddell and Leslie Gracie onto their shoulders and paraded them around the park. Everyone, even the losing team, it seemed, appreciated the skill of the two Scottish wings. In the grandstand, both the Welsh and the Scottish fans cheered.

Between running and rugby, Eric was very busy. It would have been easy for him to let his studies slide, but somehow he managed to do everything. He even managed to be in the top three students in his classes.

In 1922, after one year at home, Eric's parents' furlough came to an end, and Eric's parents returned to China with Jenny and Ernest. It was a difficult time for Eric and Robert. They had both become used to being part of a "normal" family, and it was hard for them to leave that behind and move into a hostel. Eric comforted himself with the fact that Robert would still be around for another year before he graduated as a doctor and returned to China.

Eric laughed at one piece of advice his departing mother gave him. Even though he was only twenty years old, his fine blond hair was beginning to recede, and his mother feared that his forehead would soon meet up with the small balding patch on the back of his head. No one else in the family had gone bald that young, and Eric's mother put it down to taking too many hot showers after athletics meetings and rugby games. Eric wondered what his mother thought he should do after playing rugby on a muddy field for an hour and a half.

Not only was Eric the only blond (and balding) member of his family, he was also the only one who didn't like to talk about his faith. Even his parents weren't sure what he thought about Christianity; he kept the whole matter to himself. He always went to church on Sunday, read his Bible, and lived a good life, but for some reason, he didn't feel comfortable talking to others about God. On the other hand, Robert was a very enthusiastic Christian. Not long after their parents had left for China, an evangelistic campaign was organized for all of Scotland and Robert eagerly signed up to be a part of it.

The purpose of the evangelistic campaign was to use university and high school students to share the gospel message with people all across Scotland. During their weekends and vacations, students would sleep in local churches and spend their days looking for people to invite to their nightly meetings. Many of these meetings were very successful, especially in the rural areas. The large cities, though, were much tougher. Working-class men just weren't interested in what a group of university students had to say. They were perfectly happy with their drinking, brawling, and gambling. No matter what they tried, the students couldn't seem to come up with an effective way to get their message across to these working-class people.

A group of students from the University of Glasgow moved into a church in the industrial town of Armadale, halfway between Glasgow and Edinburgh, to share the gospel message there. They, too, soon found themselves wrestling with the problem of getting their message across to working-class people. One member of this group was David Thomson, or DP, as he was known to most people. As DP thought about the problem, he had an inspiration. Like so many men in Scotland, the men of Armadale loved rugby. So DP thought that the students should challenge the local men to a game of rugby. Everyone agreed it was a good idea, and a date was set for the match. Many local men showed up for the game, and they played hard. In the end, the students narrowly won. It was a victory in other ways, too. The students made friends with a few of the men who had played in or watched the rugby game and invited them to their meetings.

DP was pleased with the success of his idea on one hand and frustrated by it on the other. Rugby was obviously a big draw for these men, but the students couldn't play games everywhere they went. A game took too long to organize, and some of the students had been hurt while playing. Yet DP felt that rugby was an important key in getting to know the local men. Then inspiration hit him again. He had been on several evangelistic campaign trips with Robert Liddell, and the two men had become friends. DP knew that Robert was a keen Christian and that his younger brother was none other than Eric Liddell, the great Scottish rugby star! If DP could persuade Robert to get Eric to speak to the men of Armadale, hundreds would turn out to hear such a famous person.

The more DP thought about the idea, the more excited he became. There was just one problem. He had never heard Robert say anything about Eric's being a Christian. Still, when DP told the other students about his idea, they, too, were enthusiastic about it. If Eric Liddell was a Christian and would come and speak, they were sure the town hall would be filled with men.

First thing the next morning, DP hitched a ride to Edinburgh. He made his way to the hostel where the Liddell brothers were living. Robert met him at the door, and DP lost no time in telling him why he had come. Robert gave DP a funny look.

"You will ask him for us, won't you?" DP asked Robert.

Robert shrugged his shoulders. "I think you'd better ask him yourself. He's out on a run right now, but he should be back soon."

As they waited for Eric to return, DP and Robert talked about how the evangelistic campaign was progressing across Scotland. After about twenty minutes, the door finally swung open and Eric strolled in. As soon as he saw a stranger sitting with Robert, he stopped and introduced himself. "Hello, I'm Eric Liddell," he said.

DP was speechless for a moment. Then his words came in a rush. "Hello, I'm David Thomson, DP for short. I'm a friend of Robert. Actually we have been on several evangelistic campaigns together."

Eric nodded as he pulled up a chair. He'd heard his brother talk about DP.

Nervously, DP spilled out his plan to Eric. When he was finished, Eric sat silently. He put his face in his hands and sighed deeply. DP began to look nervous as if he had said something that was better left unsaid.

After what seemed like an eternity, Eric finally looked up. "All right," he said. "I'll do it. Tell me where you need me and when."

Like a hinge swinging a huge door open, that simple statement forever changed the course of Eric's life. His private life was about to become very public.

Chapter 4

Something Even More Important

On April 6, 1923, Robert Liddell introduced his younger brother to eighty men who had gathered in the Armadale Town Hall. The men cheered as Eric stood up to speak. Eric shifted nervously from foot to foot. He hated being the center of attention. For a moment he just stood and said nothing. Then he took a deep breath and began. He didn't speak the way a preacher did from the pulpit or a teacher in a schoolroom. Instead he spoke quietly, as if chatting with a good friend. He spoke about how God was in control of his life and how he accepted whatever happened to him as God's best for that time. He also spoke about how much he knew God loved him and everyone sitting there in the town hall. Then he thanked them for listening and sat down.

To Eric's surprise, the next day every newspaper in Scotland carried a photo of him and a report on his talk in Armadale. The man who disliked drawing attention to himself was now more famous than ever.

Once Eric had given his first Christian speech, churches and groups everywhere began asking him to come and speak. The next week Eric found himself at another town hall, this one in Rutherglen on the outskirts of Glasgow. This time, six hundred men showed up to hear him. Eric gave them the same simple message he had presented in Armadale, told in the same simple way.

As he stood in front of the crowd in Rutherglen, Eric realized that he had been given a gift, the gift of fame, and that he could use it to share the gospel message with thousands of people. From that moment on, he was never again shy about standing in front of a crowd to speak. Indeed, he tried to accept every speaking invitation he got.

If Eric thought his life was busy before, it was hectic now. During the week he attended lectures and studied for his degree. On the weekends he would go to a track meet and arrange to speak at meetings on the way there and back. Some sports writers began writing that Eric Liddell was trying to do too much and that in the end his running would suffer. But a person had only to look at the races Eric was running in Scotland to see that that wasn't true. In fact, it seemed just the opposite; the more time Eric gave to speaking, the faster he ran.

When asked how he ran so fast, he often told people that he ran as fast as he could for the first half of a race and then asked God to help him run even faster for the second half.

Somewhere in the mind of every schoolboy or schoolgirl who has ever won a race is the tiny dream that one day he or she might win an Olympic medal. Eric had had this dream for a long time. So when the trials for the British team to attend the 1924 Olympic Games were announced, he was anxious to try out for the team. The trials were to be held in Stamford Bridge, London, in early July 1923, and the Olympics themselves were to be held in Paris exactly a year later in July 1924.

Although Eric was the best sprinter in Scotland, he wasn't automatically assured of a place on the Olympic team to represent Great Britain. Great Britain was made up of England, Northern Ireland, Scotland, and Wales, and each of these countries had its own great athletes. The only way to secure a place on the team was to be one of the first three finishers in your event at the British Championships and Olympic Trials in Stamford Bridge.

Eric did that and more! He won both heats and both finals and in the process set a new British record for the 100 yards of 9.7 seconds. (This record would stand for thirty-five years until Peter Radford bettered it by a second.) Eric finished the 220-yard race in 21.6 seconds, his best time ever over that distance. At the end of the competition, he was rewarded with the Harvey Cup for Best Athlete of the Year and, of course, something even more important to him—a place on the British Olympic team. He was entered in both the 100-meter and the 200-meter races. (The Olympic Games use metric measurements to measure the distance of the various events. A meter is approximately three inches longer than a yard.) After the team was announced, newspapers all over Great Britain blazed with stories about "Britain's best hope for a gold medal in the hundred-meter race."

The following weekend, the newspapers were announcing even more startling news. Eric had performed a "miracle"! At least, that's how it had looked to the spectators at Stoke-on-Trent. Eric was representing Scotland in a competition against Ireland and England. He was entered in the 440-yard race, a distance of once around the track. Eric hardly ever ran this distance in competitions, and he was not favored to win. He drew the inside lane, the best lane for the race. As usual, before the start of the race, he shook hands with each contestant, finishing with J. J. Gillies, a runner from England. Gillies was running in the lane next to Eric. When the starter's gun cracked, both Gillies and Eric got off to a fast start. But it took only a second for disaster to strike. J.J. Gillies, anxious to get into a good position in his lane, bumped into Eric and knocked him over the grass in the center of the track. A gasp went up from the spectators.

Gillies managed to regain his balance and keep running, but Eric lay on the grass. The race was over for him, or so he thought. He assumed he had been disqualified. Suddenly, though, he caught a glimpse of one of the officials waving frantically for him to get up. Apparently he was not disqualified, so he sprang to his feet and sprinted off down the track after the other runners, who were now at least twenty yards in front of him.

Since such races are won by inches, it seemed impossible for Eric to be able to catch up. But somehow, Eric just got faster and faster. Soon the crowd was on its feet, roaring with excitement. Was it possible that Eric could catch up to the others? Yes! He powered past the stragglers in the race. With only forty yards to go, he was in fourth place. He flung his head back even farther than normal and willed his legs to pump faster. His legs obeyed. As the runners headed down the home straight, Eric moved up until he was neck and neck with the leader. Then, with a superhuman burst of speed, he dashed across the finish line in first place.

Eric collapsed onto the track, totally exhausted. As his coach and teammates carried him off the field on a stretcher, the crowd rose to its feet and cheered on their new champion. Eric Liddell's race that day has been called the greatest quarter-mile race performance of all time.

Eric returned to a hero's welcome in Scotland. Once again, he had made the Scottish people proud, and his countrymen eagerly awaited the Olympic Games to see their hero win the gold medal in the 100 meters.

Things didn't work out quite that way, however. One morning in April 1924, three months before the start of the Olympic Games, Eric received a list of the events he was entered in. Beside each event, the times for the heats and the finals were indicated. Beside the heats for the 100-yard sprint was one fateful word: *Sunday*.

Eric stared at the page for a long time. *Sunday*. It definitely said Sunday. Eric's heat to qualify for the final would be run on a Sunday. But Eric would not run on a Sunday. There was no doubt about it in his mind. His coach and the Scottish Athletic Association already knew that he did not run races on Sundays; he never had, and he never would. Since his earliest memory, he'd been taught that Sunday was a day of rest and a day of reverence for God. All his life, Eric had honored that teaching. Sunday was God's day, and nothing, not even the promise of a gold medal, was going to sway him from that belief.

Eric informed the British Olympic Committee that he couldn't run in the 100-meter sprint. The newspapers quickly blazed out the news that Eric Liddell had refused to compete for the gold medal in the 100 meters. Now the public, who had admired him for his running ability and his character, turned on him fiercely. Some people even called him a traitor to his country, a man unfit to represent Scotland.

Eric was crushed by the cruel things people said about him, but he would not change his mind. As far as he was concerned, he would not run on Sunday, and that was all there was to it. To make matters worse, the dates for the two relay heats were posted soon afterwards. Both the 4x400-meter and the 4x100-meter relays were to be run on a Sunday. True to form, Eric refused to run in them as well.

The British Olympic Committee met privately with the organizers of the games in Paris, but it seemed there was little they could do about the scheduling of events. If a contestant refused to run on one particular day, the organizers didn't see it as their problem. Eric accepted this. It was his choice, and so, too, were the consequences of it.

Meanwhile, the British Olympic Committee decided to try to make the best of a bad situation. It asked Eric to consider running the 200-meter and 400-meter races even though he would not be favored to win a medal in either event. Eric agreed. The committee also stepped up its support of Harold Abrahams, the English runner who was still entered in the 100 meters. Harold was not as fast as Eric, but he was the best Great Britain had to offer under the circumstances.

While all this was happening, other things were going on in Eric's life. Robert had graduated from medical school and had been accepted for a position as a missionary doctor serving with the London Missionary Society in China. The brothers separated, not knowing how long it would be before they would see each other again.

After arriving in China, Robert wrote to Eric about the turmoil that the country was in the midst of. A fierce struggle for political power was going on, and as usual, it was the peasants, farmers, and poor people who suffered the most as a result. These people needed as much help as they could get. As he read the letter, Eric made a decision there and then. He decided to follow in his family's footsteps and become a missionary to China. He wasn't sure where he should go in China, so he made plans to go first to Tientsin, where he had been born and where his parents were now stationed. There he could live with his family while he got established. Quietly, without telling anyone, he wrote away to the Anglo-Chinese college in Tientsin to ask if they needed the services of a science teacher or a sports coach. He knew as he posted the letter that he would have to wait several months for a reply. This was fine with him, because he had a lot to do while he waited.

To allow him to attend the Olympics and still graduate on schedule, Eric's professors had let him hand in assignments ahead of time. This, however, meant a lot of extra work for Eric, not to mention keeping up his training for the games. Finally, all the hard work was behind him, and Eric joined the British Olympic team for the voyage across the English Channel to Paris. On board the boat, many of the other athletes on the team privately told Eric that they admired his stand against running on Sunday. Eric appreciated their support, even if they didn't express it out loud to the press.

Saturday, July 5, 1924, was a very hot day Paris. It was also the day the Eighth Olympic Games of modern times were officially opened. The Olympic Games had originated in Athens, Greece, in 776 B.C. to honor the twelve gods (especially Zeus, the most powerful of them all) who, according to myth, lived on Mount Olympus. The games were held every four years and consisted of a day of running races and wrestling matches. Eventually, in A.D. 393, they were banned by Roman Emperor Theodoseus. At the end of the nineteenth century, a Frenchman, Baron Pierre de Courbetin, made it his mission to bring back the Olympic Games. This time, every country in the world would be invited to send contestants, and many sports would be played. The idea caught on, and in 1896, the first of the modern Olympic Games was opened in Athens. The games had been held every four years since then, except for 1916, when they were canceled because of World War I.

Over the years, several changes were made to the games. The 1912 Olympic Games in Stockholm, Sweden, were the first to allow women to compete, and the 1924 Paris Olympics were the first to include winter sports. (Of course, the winter events were not held in the sweltering summer heat of Paris. They were held in the French Alps at Chamonix.)

Each country also had its own rules about entering the games. The United States poured a lot of money into helping its contestants. The U.S. government hired an ocean liner, the USS *America,* to take the U.S. team to the Olympics. The ship had a special 200-meter cork track installed on board so that the athletes could continue their training. Once in Paris, the American team had the best accommodations and plenty of money to pay twice or even three times the going rate for a taxi. Because of this, the other teams often found it difficult to get a taxi to take them to Colombe Stadium where the games were being held. If they weren't Americans, the taxi drivers didn't seem interested in taking them. Many of the other contestants often had to resort to flagging down private cars and begging for a ride to the stadium to compete in their event.

Nineteen twenty-four was also the first year the British government helped its competitors pay for their travel and accommodations. Until this time, each competitor had paid all his or her own expenses to compete in the games. It was a good thing that the British government had decided to change this, because Eric would never have been able to come up with the money necessary to cover his expenses.

During the opening ceremony, Eric marched proudly into Colombe Stadium with the rest of the British team. The Union Jack fluttered lightly over them. The team was dressed in blue and white, the women with white skirts and blue blazers and the men with white pants and the same blue blazers. The men also wore white straw hats. The drone of bagpipes played by the king's own pipers filled the air as the athletes marched in. Each male member of the team took off his hat as a sign of respect as the team passed the podium where the French president and Baron Pierre de Courbetin stood watching. One by one the rest of the teams marched into the stadium until all forty-five teams were lined up side by side in the center of the field. Some teams were huge. The U.S. team alone had over four hundred competitors. On the other hand, China had sent only two athletes, and Haiti one. The lone Haitian had to carry his own flag as well as be the entire team!

As the hot afternoon sun beat down, the opening ceremony began. Baron Pierre de Courbetin declared the games open, cannons boomed, thousands of pigeons were released, and the Olympic flag was hoisted into the hot, stagnant air. The sixty thousand spectators cheered. The 1924 Olympic Games had officially begun.

As the teams were about to march out of the stadium, Lord Cadogan, head of the British Olympic Committee, strolled over to the British team and wished the members all luck. As he moved among the team members shaking their hands, he stopped right in front of Eric and in a loud voice declared, "To play the game is the only thing in life that matters." Lord Cadogan looked directly at Eric as he spoke, and Eric got the point. Eric Liddell had thrown away a gold medal for Britain, and there were many who would never forgive him for it. As a result, Eric left the stadium that day a little less excited than when he'd arrived. But he still marched out with his head held high. No one, not even an English nobleman, could tell him a game was the most important thing in his life. It wasn't.

Eric didn't care what people thought of his decision. Yet he was also determined to do his best in the races he was entered in and would wait and see what the outcome was. The outcome would be worth every bit of effort he had put forth.

Chapter 5

Against All Odds

The day after the opening ceremony was Sunday, not just any Sunday, but the Sunday Eric had refused to run on. Harold Abrahams, a student at Cambridge University, lined up with the other contestants to try to qualify for the 100-meter finals for Great Britain. Meanwhile, Eric Liddell was nowhere to be seen. Eric was at the Scots Kirk (church) across town. As the heats for the 100-meter sprint were being raced, Eric was giving one of his talks to the congregation. When he came out of church, he heard the good news that Harold Abrahams had won his heat and was entered in the final the following day.

Eric was thrilled at the news. Maybe Great Britain would get her gold after all. And that is just what happened. The next day, Eric was in the stadium cheering for Harold Abrahams as Harold streaked past the field and won in a great time—10.6 seconds. Harold was the first European ever to win a gold medal in the event. Eric clapped and whistled along with everyone else. As the Union Jack was raised over Colombes Stadium and "God Save the King" was played, Eric stood proudly watching as the gold medal was hung around Harold Abrahams' neck. But along with national pride, Eric felt a tinge of sadness. Perhaps it could have been he standing there receiving the medal. Yet he didn't regret his decision not to run on a Sunday. Of course, the fact that Great Britain had won the desired gold medal helped him feel better about things. At last, he hoped, the press would stop printing horrible stories about him and he could finally concentrate on the events he would be running in.

That night Eric slept soundly at the Hotel du Louvre, and he was up early the next morning to make sure he got a ride to the stadium in time for his race. Already several athletes in Paris for the games had endured the heartbreaking situation of not finding a taxi or a private car willing to take them to the stadium in time for them to compete in their events.

Eric made it to the stadium in plenty of time. He strolled out of the dressing room clad in the British track uniform—baggy white shorts that flapped around his knees and a white top with short sleeves.

He began to limber up for the qualifying heat for the 200-meter race. Harold Abrahams was running in the same heat. Finally, the runners were called to the starting line. As soon as the starting pistol sounded, Eric and Harold streaked down the track, and they both qualified for the final. People who knew a lot about running, though, gave neither Eric nor Harold much hope of ending up among the first three finishers in the final. The American runners in the final were the hot favorites to win all the medals.

As Eric Liddell and Harold Abrahams lined up for the 200-meter final, four other men were lined up beside them. All four were from the United States. When the starter's gun cracked, the other runners got off to a great start. Eric, however, was slow off the mark. But in the dash for the finish line, he managed to overtake Harold Abrahams and two of the Americans. The other two Americans had crossed the line ahead of him, but Eric had won the bronze medal for Great Britain. Harold Abrahams had finished last.

The result of the 200-meter final left no doubt in anyone's mind that the Americans were the best runners at the games and would likely win the other events as well, especially the 400-meter race. However, there was a rumor that the Swiss had a strong runner entered in the 400 meters who might be able to challenge for a medal. Great Britain might have had a chance at winning a medal if Guy Butler had not hurt his leg just before the games. Butler had won a silver medal in the event at the Antwerp Games in 1920. The British coaches had bandaged up his injured leg so that he could run, but it was too painful for him to crouch at the start of the race. Guy Butler would have to start from a standing position, making it very unlikely that he could win a medal. Eric was also entered in the race, but 400 meters wasn't his normal race distance, and no one gave him any chance of winning a medal.

The heats for the 400-meter race were held on Thursday, the hottest day so far at the games. The temperature rose to 45 degrees Celcius (113 degrees Fahrenheit). The heat didn't normally bother Eric. Like most runners, he liked the hot weather because it tended to make the muscles soft and flexible. But this weather was almost too hot to run in. The 10,000-meter cross-country race had been run earlier in the day, and of the thirty-eight runners who started the race, only twenty-three had made it to the finish line. The rest had collapsed from heat exhaustion along the route. The newspapers had quickly dubbed Colombes Stadium "The Cauldron," and on this day it seemed a fitting nickname.

Despite the fact that no one expected him to do well, Eric threw all his energy into the race and managed to squeak into the finals. Amazingly, so did Guy Butler. The best qualifier in their heat, though, turned out to be the Swiss runner Joseph Imbach, who had stunned everyone by breaking the world record for the race during the heat. Imbach ran 400 meters in 48 seconds. People were enthusiastic about his chances for winning the gold medal, that is, until the American runner Horatio Fitch topped Imbach by winning his heat in 47.8 seconds!

The final was set for 7 P.M. Friday, July 11. Since a new 400-meter record had been set twice in the heats, the crowd began to gather early for the race. Eric took one of the few taxis the Americans weren't using to the stadium around 4 P.M. In his pocket was a note that had been sent to his hotel room that read, "In the old book it says, 'He who honors me, I will honor.' Wishing you the best of success always." It was signed by the masseur for the British team, and it meant a lot to Eric. Even if most people didn't understand why he chose not to run on a Sunday, some did. As Eric walked into the stadium, he reached into his pocket and rested his hand on the note. Whatever happened in the final of the 400 meters, Eric knew he had honored God first, and that was worth more than any Olympic medal.

By quarter till seven, six runners were milling around the starting line: Horatio Fitch and Conrad Taylor representing the United States, Joseph Imbach of Switzerland, David Johnson of Canada, and the two British finalists, Guy Butler and Eric Liddell. As usual, Eric shook each runner's hand and wished the runners success in the race. Spectators couldn't help but notice Eric who, at 5′ 9″, was the shortest of the six runners. Again, anyone who knew anything about running would have known that to be good in the 400 meters, a runner needed to be tall. Eric might be a good sprinter, but for this distance, longer legs were a definite advantage.

Several minutes before the race was due to start, the runners drew numbers for the lane they would run in. Eric's heart sank as he pulled out a card with the number six on it. This meant he would be in the outside lane of the track. He would start slightly in front of the others and gradually lose that advantage as the track curved. It meant that Eric wouldn't be able to see where any of the other runners were unless they were beating him. The track at Colombes Stadium was longer than most. Since it was 500 meters around, the 400-meter race would take the runners around only one of the bends in the track, with the race finishing 100 meters short of the starting line. This made running in the outside lane very difficult.

Eric took his trowel from the leather pouch he carried with him, placed his feet where he wanted them to be when he started, and made marks with his toes. Then he used the trowel to dig two small holes for his toes where he had marked. He could hear the familiar drone of bagpipes. As he glanced around, he saw the king's pipers marching proudly around the inside of the track, playing a traditional Scottish tune, "The Campbells Are Coming." Eric smiled and waved to them as he put his trowel back in the leather pouch and handed it to his coach. He was the only Scotsman in the finals, and he knew the pipers were playing for him.

Suddenly, the bagpipe music faded, and the runners were called to their marks. Eric crouched at the starting line. In admiration, he glanced over at Guy Butler, who was again starting from a standing position. As he waited for the only sound that now mattered, the crack of the starter's pistol, Eric could feel every muscle in his body tense.

When the pistol sounded, Eric lunged forward. He threw his head back and assumed his strange running position. His feet beat against the cinder track as he gathered speed down the back straight. As he rounded the bend in the track, the point where the runners would bunch up together, he expected to see Horatio Fitch and Joseph Imbach out in front of him. After all, they had both set new world records for the distance during their heats. When they weren't out in front, Eric threw his head back even farther and willed his legs to go even faster.

In less than a minute, it was all over, and Eric was the first across the finish line. Against all odds, he had won!

Eric collapsed into the arms of the British coach, totally exhausted. It was several minutes before he realized that not only had he won but also he had set a new world record of 47.6 seconds for the distance. He had broken the record Horatio Fitch had set in his heat by two-tenths of a second. Horatio Fitch, himself, had finished a distant second in the race, and somehow Guy Butler had managed to fend off the other three runners to finish in third place.

After he had regained his strength, Eric climbed onto the top position of the stand where the gold medal was draped around his neck. To his right was Horatio Fitch, and to his left, Guy Butler. Above them the Union Jack flapped in the breeze at the top of the flagpole. Below it was the Stars and Stripes of the United States, and then another Union Jack. After the other two runners had received their medals, the band struck up "God Save the King," the national anthem of Great Britain. A smile brimmed across Eric's face. Now Great Britain had another gold medal, and one she hadn't expected to win. All around him the crowd cheered.

After it was all over, Eric slipped quietly away from the crowd and headed to the dressing room. Quickly he showered and changed clothes. He wanted to get back to the hotel as soon as possible. He'd agreed to speak at the Scots Kirk again on Sunday, and he needed time to prepare what he was going to say.

The next morning, Saturday, the applause that had been heard all over Paris after Eric's win was now resounding throughout Scotland. The newspapers that had been so critical of him when he would not run in the 100-meter sprint on Sunday were now trying to outdo each other in praising him. *The Scotsman* reported, "Certainly there has not been a more popular win. The crowd went into a frenzy of enthusiasm." The Edinburgh *Evening News* wrote, "All around the banked area people were on their feet cheering madly, and as if by magic, hosts of Union Jacks appeared over the heads of the raving crowd as Liddell ripped through the tape and into the arms of the Britishers who were waiting for him." *The Bulletin,* another Scottish newspaper, reported that Eric Liddell's win was "the greatest achievement in the Olympic Games so far."

Eric was amused when he read the accounts in the newspapers. One day he was a coward and traitor to Scotland; the next he was being hailed as a national hero.

As he watched the remaining days of the Paris Olympic Games, one thought was never far from Eric's mind. How would the Scottish people react when they found out that their top sports star was about to buy a one-way ticket to China? What would the newspapers say about him then?

Chapter 6

Local Hero

Eric peered out the train window. The train was approaching Victoria Station. Soon the members of the 1924 British Olympic team would separate and go their own ways. Eric would be returning to Edinburgh, where he was due to graduate from university the following Saturday. As the train pulled slowly into the station, people ran along the platform from carriage to carriage looking in the windows.

"He's in here," yelled a teenage boy as he pointed at Eric.

Soon a mob of people was gathered outside the carriage Eric that was riding in. The crowd began cheering "We want Eric. We want Eric." As Eric gingerly opened the carriage door, a flood of cheers greeted him. Several of the men in the crowd grabbed him. He felt himself being hoisted onto their shoulders. The crowd went wild, cheering as Eric was paraded around the platform.

Finally, things died down enough for Eric to make his way to a friend's home to stay the night. The following day, Eric set off for Edinburgh. It was not an easy trip. People everywhere recognized him. Young boys would thrust autograph books at him, and old men wanted to shake his hand or slap him on the back. Even though Eric was shy by nature, he did not mind the attention too much. He realized he had won his medals for the people of the British Isles. Now those people wanted to congratulate him. Still, he was glad when he finally arrived home in Edinburgh.

The following Saturday, Eric donned his black robe with its wide hood ready to receive his bachelor of science degree. (Scottish graduates wear a hood, not a mortarboard, as do graduating students in many other countries.) Eric took his place in alphabetical order in the front row of McEwan Hall, where the graduation ceremony was to take place. He listened closely as Vice-Chancellor Sir Alfred Ewing gave the commencement address. Then, one by one, the graduating students were called up to receive their degrees. The audience applauded each student. They got to the "Ls." First, Lambert, G.H.; then Lemont, F.M.; and finally, Liddell, E.H.

As Eric stood, so did everyone else in McEwan Hall. The crowd cheered and clapped as Eric stepped onto the stage. Sir Alfred Ewing raised his hand, motioning the crowd to be quiet, but no one took the slightest notice of him. The people cheered and clapped and stomped their feet for several minutes before quieting down enough for the vice-chancellor to make a short speech. The speech was even shorter than he had planned. Sir Alfred Ewing barely had time to say, "Well, Mr. Liddell, you have shown that no one can pass you but the examiner," when the applause erupted again.

A full minute later, the crowd again quieted down and Sir Alfred Ewing was able to go on. He explained how in the ancient Olympics the champions were crowned with wreaths made from laurel leaves. As he spoke, he reached under the podium and pulled out a wreath. "Now, I was not able to obtain Greek laurel leaves here in Scotland, but the head gardener at the Royal Botanical Gardens assures me this is as close as we will find." With that, he placed the wreath firmly on Eric's head. Then the Greek master, who was also on stage, stepped forward and began to read a poem that he had written about Eric's victory. The poem was in ancient Greek, and Eric didn't understand much of it, but it sounded very grand!

Finally, Eric was handed his bachelor of science degree. He gave the audience a smile and a wave and headed off the stage. It was not until he had sat down again that the applause finally died away and the ceremony could go on.

After the ceremony, there was to be a church service at St. Giles Cathedral on High Street. Eric had expected to walk there like everyone else, but that didn't happen. As soon as Sir Alfred Ewing had thanked everyone for coming, Eric's fellow students surged toward Eric. Before he knew what was happening, Eric was hoisted onto a chair with poles nailed to either side of it so that it could be carried on the shoulders of his fellow students. Soon the chair was lifted above the crowd, and Eric was carried from McEwan Hall, down the steps, and all the way to the cathedral.

Eric was still wearing the wreath when the students finally deposited him on the front steps of the cathedral. Suddenly the crowd that had accompanied him from the university was silent. Eric realized that it was waiting for him to give a speech.

In an instant, his mind flashed back to his fellow athletes who had tried their hardest for Great Britain but had not come back from Paris as Olympic champions. As he thought about them, Eric remembered a quote he'd read somewhere. He repeated the quote for the crowd. "In the dust of defeat as well as the laurels of victory there is glory to be found if one has done his best." Then he talked for a few minutes about what the words meant, reminding the crowd that they should all be proud of themselves when they know they've tried their hardest at something.

During the service in the cathedral, Eric sat quietly and listened to the sermon. He had hoped that things would have died down by the time the service was over, but the other students had an even bigger surprise for him. When the service was over, Eric was led down the aisle and through the double wooden doors. As he walked out into the sunlight, he saw a horse-drawn carriage waiting.

Before he had time to realize what was happening, Eric found himself sitting inside the carriage next to Sir Alfred Ewing. The carriage pulled off and traveled along the Royal Mile and onto Princes Street, Edinburgh's main street. All along the way, huge crowds had gathered to honor their local sports hero. Eric smiled and waved to them. Finally, the carriage stopped outside the vice-chancellor's home, and Eric was invited in for dinner.

It had been a wonderful day, and Eric happily wrote and told his parents and Robert all about it. He wished they could have seen it for themselves. Since they hadn't, he sent them a pile of newspaper clippings about his achievements in Paris at the Olympic Games.

The celebrations did not end in a single day, though. For the next week, receptions and parties were held for Eric every day. Just when Eric thought he could take no more, it was time for him to climb aboard the train for a trip to London. There, at Stamford Bridge, he was to compete for the British Empire against the United States. It had been arranged before the Olympic Games started that the American team would stop off in London on its way home for the competition. As he rumbled along on the train towards London, Eric could hardly believe it had been only eight days since the Olympic Games had ended. So much had happened to him in such a short time.

Eric was to be the last man (the anchor) on the British Empire's 4x400-meter relay team. The anchor on the American team was none other than Horatio Fitch, whom Eric had beaten in the final of the 400-meter race in Paris. Everyone present for the competition wondered whether Eric could beat Fitch again. The people didn't have to wait long to find out.

As the runners rounded the turn, just before handing off their batons to the anchors, it was obvious that the United States should win the relay. As Eric Liddell reached back and grabbed the baton from his British teammate, he was a full seven meters behind Horatio Fitch. Eric threw his head back and thrashed his arms back and forth at his side in his odd running style. As he did so, he gathered speed. By the time he reached the first turn, Eric was gaining on Horatio Fitch. Down the back straight he pulled even with him. But on the second turn, Horatio managed to hold off Eric's challenge and stay just in front, though not by much. But as they entered the home straight and headed for the finish line, Horatio Fitch had no answer for Eric's final burst of speed. Eric began to pull away and crossed the finish line four meters ahead of Horatio Fitch. The crowd went wild.

By the time Eric got back to Scotland, everyone had heard about his latest victory. More people than ever wanted to hold parties in his honor. For the time being, he was Scotland's greatest sports star.

A week after arriving back in Edinburgh, Eric was at yet another dinner in his honor. This time he had invited his old coach, Tom McKerchar, to attend with him. During his speech, Eric told the audience how much Tom McKerchar had helped and encouraged him when he had been a green athlete fresh out of high school. When the speech was over, the crowd clapped and cheered. Tom McKerchar stood and bowed and then sat down again. Everyone expected Eric to do the same. But as the applause died away, Eric continued to stand with a serious look fixed on his face. The audience grew silent. Did Eric Liddell have something else to say?

Eric cleared his throat and began softly. "Before I sit down, there is one more thing I would like to tell you all. It has been a wonderful experience to compete in the Olympic Games and to bring home a gold medal. But since I have been a young lad, I have had my eyes on a different prize. You see, each one of us is in a greater race than any I have run in Paris, and this race ends when God gives out the medals. It has always been my intention to be a missionary, and I have just received word that I have been accepted as a chemistry teacher at the Anglo-Chinese college in Tientsin, China. From now on, I will be putting my energy into preparing to take up that position."

The room was completely silent. People stared at Eric with open mouths; the impact of what he had just said was slowly sinking in. Scotland's greatest athlete was giving up running to go to China! Within hours, every newspaper in the country would carry the stunning news.

Eric was glad the news was finally out. Now everyone knew of his decision, and he could busy himself making plans to get to China. While he looked forward to teaching chemistry and being a coach at the college, more than just teaching and coaching students, Eric wanted to help them spiritually. But to be more effective doing that he felt he needed some extra training. After communicating futher with the Anglo-Chinese college in Tientsin, it was decided that he should stay one more year in Scotland and study theology at the Congregational college in Edinburgh.

Of course, study did not keep Eric, being who he was, busy all the time. Eric managed to fit in several extensive Christian speaking tours during that year. He toured England several times, and everywhere he went, huge crowds turned out to hear him. He also traveled to Germany, where the British Army still occupied tracts of the Rhineland it had captured during World War I.

Everything Eric did, whether taking part in a charity run or playing a fun game of rugby, was written about in the newspapers the following day. Nothing about him seemed too trivial to report on. People all over Scotland seemed to want to read about everything Eric was up to. Elsa McKechnie was one such person. She was a fourteen-year-old girl who followed what Eric was doing with great interest. Every night she would scour the newspapers to see if there was anything new to read about him. She would discuss all she found out about Eric with her friends at the George Watson Ladies College in Edinburgh. Nearly all the girls at the school had the same interest in Eric as Elsa. He was, after all, a local hero, not to mention a very charming young man.

One day Elsa McKechnie had an idea. Why not form an Eric Liddell Fan Club? She discussed the idea with her friends at school, and they all agreed it would be a great thing to do. Elsa quickly made up rules for the new club. To become a member, a person had to pass an oral exam about the life of Eric Liddell. Once a person passed the test, she was entitled to use one page of the club's scrapbook to write down a poem or some thoughts on Eric. In return, the members were each given a photo of Eric which they promised to display in a place of honor.

Elsa McKechnie wrote to Eric to tell him about the fan club and ask whether he would give his permission to make it the *official* Eric Liddell Fan Club. She even asked him to come to dinner at her house. As soon as Eric got her letter, he wrote to Elsa, giving her permission to run the one and only Official Eric Liddell Fan Club and accepting her invitation to dinner.

Elsa was too excited to say much during the meal, but she watched everything Eric did and tried to remember every word he said so that she could report to the other members of the club at a special meeting she had called for the following day. When Eric left the house after dinner, Elsa drained the rest of the tea from the cup he had been drinking from and dried the tea leaves left in the bottom. She tucked them inside an envelope. They became one of her most prized possessions. Such was the impression Eric Liddell left on young girls in Scotland!

Time was passing quickly, though. Before Eric knew it, his year at the Congregational college was over, and he was packing for China. Newspapers counted down the weeks until July 13. One paper even printed a cartoon of Eric running in black shorts and a clergyman's collar! Many people in Scotland understood why he was leaving, and they wanted to encourage him any way they could. Eric's last official running event was at the Scottish AAA Championships at Hampden Park, Glasgow. When people heard that Eric Liddell was entered in the 100-, 220-, and 440-yard races, twelve thousand spectators showed up to cheer him on. Eric thrilled his fans by winning all three races.

Not only did Eric's admirers come to see him run one last time before he left Scotland, but enormous crowds came to hear him speak in churches as well. As many as a thousand people had to be turned away sometimes because there was no more room in the church where he was speaking. When the time came for him to leave, there was hardly a person in all Scotland who didn't know where Eric was going and why. Just as when he had returned from the Olympic Games in Paris, an endless round of luncheons and dinners was arranged for people to say good-bye to Eric, who graciously attended them all.

Finally, Monday, July 13, 1925, arrived. At 5 P.M. Eric picked up his suitcases and looked around his room one last time. His friends had arranged for him to get to Waverley Railway Station, but they had given him no details about the arrangements. As Eric opened the door and stepped out into the warm evening, his mouth fell open in shock. In front of him was a carriage, much like the one that had taken him from St. Giles Cathedral to the vice-chancellor's house for dinner a year ago. However, this carriage was different in one big way. Instead of being drawn by two horses like the previous carriage, this carriage was led by two teams of students and friends, who held the shaft in their hands, ready to pull the carriage with Eric in it all the way to the station.

Amid cheering and whistling, Eric climbed into the carriage, and off the men trotted. The teams pulled the carriage up Hope Terrace, along Clerk Street and then Nicholson Street, over the bridge, and on to the station. All along the route, people had gathered to say farewell to Scotland's most famous and well-loved athlete. Some people even burst into tears as Eric passed by; others waved and whistled loudly. Traffic ground to a halt as the crowd surged forward for one last glimpse of their hero. Drivers honked their car horns and counted themselves lucky to be caught in a traffic jam caused by people wanting to honor Eric Liddell.

Finally, the carriage arrived at the station, and Eric began a torturous round of good-byes. No one was sure when they would see him again, and so many people wanted to shake his hand and wish him well that it was impossible to get to everyone.

As the train puffed into the station, the crowd began to sing hymns, and Eric joined in with them. He was still singing as he climbed aboard and found himself a seat. He pulled the window open and began to wave to everyone. As he waved good-bye to his friends and said good-bye to his life in Edinburgh, he knew he was saying good-bye to something else, too. From now on, he would no longer be living in a country where he was a national hero and recognized in every corner store. He was about to become a stranger in a strange and troubled land.

Chapter 7

A Troubled Land

Eric settled into his seat for the trip to London. As the train rattled along, he began catching up on his reading. He especially wanted to reread some of the letters his father had written him about what to expect when he got to Tientsin. The letters were not lighthearted but told of the huge problems facing China in 1925.

Eric's father told about the waves of fighting and revolution that had swept over the country in the eighteen years since Eric had left China as a five-year-old. In 1911, the Qing Dynasty, which had ruled China for two hundred sixty-seven years, collapsed. Following its collapse, a new Republic of China was declared, and a new government was set up. But the new government was wracked with divisions and turmoil. So, like many other times in Chinese history when there wasn't a strong government in control, local warlords, using their private armies, began to exert their control over certain areas. For several years now, these local warlords and other political factions had been locked in a bitter struggle for control of China.

Eric's father had written that there were basically three groups involved in the struggle. There were the local warlords, the Nationalists, or the Kuomintang, as they called themselves, and a new group, the Communists, who patterned themselves after the Bolsheviks, who had seized power in Russia and transformed that country into the Soviet Union. The Kuomintang was the largest and most powerful group and found most of its support in the cities. It was also recognized as the rightful government of China, though it by no means controlled the country. The Communists were a small but growing group, and most of their support came from the rural areas in the south of China. As these different factions fought for control in various regions, it was not uncommon for some villages to change hands between a warlord, the Communists, and the Nationalists five or six times a year. Each time an army passed through a village, the village's occupants had their homes robbed and their food supplies stolen. When an army marched through the countryside, it would steal the crops from the field and trample those not ready to harvest so that the other groups couldn't get their hands on them. This in turn had led to famine.

Apart from the fighting itself, China's other enemy was foreign influence. The people of China had been humiliated by the British during the First Opium War of 1839–42. China had many goods that Great Britain wanted to trade for, but the Chinese wanted nothing except silver from the British in return for them. When the British tried to force opium on the Chinese instead of silver as payment for the goods they wanted, the emperor had refused. He ordered all opium destroyed. This in turn angered the British, who began a war with China. The British easily won, and China was forced to sign a treaty to end the war. Not only did the treaty allow the British to import opium into China, but it also opened up a number of coastal cities where foreigners could live and trade. The treaty left the Chinese people feeling weak, powerless, and very angry.

Once China had been weakened, its neighbor, Japan, saw a great opportunity to expand. In the Sino-Japanese War of 1894–95, China had lost control of Taiwan completely as well as most of its influence over the Korean Peninsula.

In 1914, three years after the collapse of the Qing Dynasty, World War I began in Europe. China eventually sided with the Allies (Great Britain, France and, Russia) against Germany and the Austro-Hungarian Empire. In joining with the Allies, China had hoped to be taken seriously as a nation and gain some respect as a country when the war was over. However, things did not work out that way. At the Treaty of Versailles, which officially ended

World War I, the Allies completely ignored China's demand that in return for fighting in the war, foreign powers should pull out of the country and leave China to govern herself.

The people of China were furious at this result. They felt they had been betrayed by the Allies. This, in turn, led to even more bitterness towards foreigners than had existed before the war. To the Chinese, foreigners, along with their ways of doing things, were symbols of China's humiliation.

It was to this China that Eric Liddell, now twenty-three, would be returning. His father's letters made it clear to Eric that unlike when he was a small boy with lots of Chinese friends, he would not be welcome in many Chinese homes, and sometimes his life might even be in danger. Despite the warning, Eric was determined to go. He felt that God had called him to work in China, and he was prepared for whatever might happen to him while he was there.

When Eric had left China as a child, the only way to get to and from England was by ship. Now, in 1925, the Trans-Siberian Railway rolled across western Russia, over the Ural Mountains, and across Siberia, finally ending in Vladivostok on the Pacific coast. In eastern Siberia, a line branched off from the Trans-Siberian Railway and headed south into China. It was possible to board a train in The Hague, Holland, and go overland all the way across Europe and Asia to Tientsin, China. That was the route Eric chose. From London he took a boat to Holland, where he caught the train. Two weeks later, the train was rolling along in China.

Eric did not go all the way to Tientsin right away, however. The railway passed through the seaside town of Pei-tia-ho, where Eric's entire family was waiting for him. They were all on vacation there together and thought it would be a good idea for Eric to join them for six weeks before traveling on to Tientsin to prepare for the new school year.

It was late afternoon when the train finally pulled to a stop at the station in Pei-tia-ho. Eric clambered onto the platform and into the welcoming arms of his family. He was thrilled to be seeing his parents, Jenny, Ernest, and Robert again; and he was especially glad to meet Robert's new wife.

The family stayed up very late that night swapping stories with Eric about what had happened to them since they had last seen each other. They were especially anxious for Eric to tell them all about what it was like to run and win a gold medal in the Olympic Games.

There was one matter, though, that James Liddell decided to leave until the next morning to discuss. Over several cups of hot tea the following morning, he broke the news to his son that there were no students to teach the following year at the Anglo-Chinese college. All five hundred of them had gone on strike!

It had all begun in Shanghai when a group of Chinese workers at a Japanese-owned cotton mill had been fired. All of the other Chinese workers at the mill had gone on strike in support of their fired co-workers. Students in Shanghai had decided to hold a demonstration to support the workers, but their demonstration had turned into a nightmare. British Colonial forces, who protected the British quarter of Shanghai (or British concession, as it was known), fired on the Chinese students and striking workers. One demonstrator was killed in the shooting.

The event became known as the "May 30th Massacre," and news of it spread quickly throughout China. Students and workers went on strike all along the eastern coast of China, and Tientsin, with its large foreign population, was a natural target for such a strike. The Anglo-Chinese college was one of the first places in Tientsin to empty out. Students there were made to feel ashamed at going to a school where five of the thirty teachers were from England and where the English language was taught. Soon they stopped showing up for class, and the school had closed early for the year.

Over the next few days, Eric met most of the other English teachers from his new school. The teachers were all vacationing in Pei-tia-ho. Most mission organizations seemed to have vacation cottages there. At picnics and over games of tennis, the teachers discussed the situation among themselves. Eventually, they decided to open the school as usual in September and wait to see whether any of their Chinese students came back to enroll for the new year.

Eric, who had forgotten nearly all the Chinese he'd spoken so well as a small child, set about studying the language while in Pei-tia-ho. Soon he found himself remembering more and more Chinese words and phrases.

Surprisingly, Eric also knew most of the missionaries vacationing in Pei-tia-ho. Many of them had stayed in London and visited their sons at Eltham College. Others had visited Eric in Edinburgh when they were home on furlough. In fact, there was only one family there he had not seen before—the McKenzies from Canada, who had two daughters, Florence and Margaret.

After six wonderful weeks in Pei-tia-ho with his family, Eric boarded the train again for the final leg of his journey to Tientsin. He needed to prepare for his classes in case any of the students decided to return to school. The rest of his family, except his father, stayed on a little longer in Pei-tia-ho. James Liddell traveled back to Tientsin with his son to keep him company.

Eric's first glance of the city where he had been born was through the window of the train. Tientsin was alive with activity. Everyone seemed to be on the move: Bicycles, rickshaws, electric streetcars, pedestrians, and motorcars all jostled for space on the narrow paved roads.

At the station in Tientsin, James Liddell hired two rickshaws. The drivers quickly stowed their passengers' suitcases on the back of the rickshaws and helped Eric and his father get seated. On their way back to the house, James Liddell had the drivers detour past the docks.

Although Tientsin was thirty miles up the Haiho River from the Yellow Sea, it was a sprawling, bustling port that serviced Peking, one hundred miles farther inland. The docks fascinated Eric. They seemed to go on for miles, and everything imaginable was being unloaded from the barges that had come up the river.

Surrounding the docks were hovels where the workers lived. Eric had seen overcrowded housing conditions in London and Edinburgh, but nothing like this. It was hard to describe the dwellings as houses. They were ramshackle shacks packed so close together it was hard for people to move between them.

As the rickshaw drivers trotted on, they passed through a police checkpoint, and Eric's father yelled to Eric that they had entered the French concession. This meant that French policemen patrolled the streets and French, not Chinese, law had to be obeyed there. As they entered the concession, the slums instantly gave way to beautiful white mansions with swimming pools and tennis courts nestled along stately, tree-lined streets. For some reason, which no one could remember by 1925, the homes used by missionaries of the London Missionary Society were all located in the French concession. At James Liddell's instruction, the rickshaw driver stopped outside number 6, London Mission Street.

Eric whistled as he climbed down from the rickshaw. "This is some house you have here, Father," he commented as he looked up at the four-story mansion.

"We lived in a much smaller one until the London Missionary Society found out you were going to be living with us. Then they insisted we move into this monstrosity," said his father in his thick Scottish accent. "Still, with the amount of entertaining your mother does, it will be filled with people in no time."

Eric smiled. He knew what his father meant. His mother was always inviting people over for a meal or to stay for a few days. "Aye, the house will be well used, that's for certain," he replied, helping his father with their suitcases.

The house was as impressive inside as it was outside. On the ground floor were the kitchen and dining room and his father's study. The living areas were on the second floor, and all the bedrooms and bathrooms were located on the third floor. There were two empty bedrooms for Eric to choose from, but instead, he kept climbing the stairs. The whole top floor was attic rooms, each with a sloped ceiling. All of the attic rooms were used for storage. Eric strolled over to the attic window that overlooked the tennis court in the backyard. "This will do me fine," he said, looking around at the boxes that would have to be moved to another room.

It didn't take Eric long to get the boxes moved and to set up his belongings in the new room. Most of his suitcases were filled with books about religion or science.

Eric was eager to see the Anglo-Chinese college. First thing the following morning he made his way to the school. He stood outside the gates staring at the huge gray stone building. He had been told that the school was called the "Eton of China," after the famous private school in England. Eric could see why. It looked just like an English school, but it was right in the center of a Chinese city! Eric swung the iron gate open and walked up the cobblestone path to the wide stone stairs flanked on either side by potted plants. He climbed the stairs and rang the doorbell. The door was quickly opened by a Chinese woman who spoke perfect English. Eric introduced himself to her and asked whether any of the other staff were around. The Chinese woman told him to wait. Moments later, the school principal came to the door. "Dr. Lavington Hart. Come in," he said in a booming voice, thrusting out his hand to shake Eric's.

"Eric Liddell, Sir. Pleased to meet you," Eric responded as the two men shook hands.

"How about a tour of the place?" asked Dr. Hart. "I expect you want to see what you've signed up for." He laughed as he patted Eric on the back and motioned him outside again.

The first place Dr. Hart took Eric was to the sports field. On the way there, he explained why he had started the school twenty-three years before. "When I came to China," he said, "all the missionaries were concentrating on reaching the very poorest people with the gospel message. Of course, that's wonderful, but no one seemed to have thought of the rich people, the politicians, lawyers, doctors, and university professors. No one was sharing the gospel message with them. I began to think it was these people, the rich and influential, who were going to lead China into the future. I began to wonder what would happen if some of these future leaders were Christians. So I set up the school for the sons of rich and influential Chinese people. Many of the boys who've been through the school have become Christians, and they have gone on to universities here and overseas and then to important positions all over China."

Eric nodded. "Yes," he said, "I remember several of them coming to talk to us when I was at Eltham College in London."

"Then you know the quality of young men we are turning out here. And sports are a big part of it," said Dr. Hart with a flourish as they turned the corner at the back of the buildings and reached the sports field. "In fact," he went on, "we were the first school in North China to begin a sports and physical education program. You should have been here the first few years when we were trying to get this all off the ground. Looking back, it's rather funny, but at the time it was very difficult."

"Why was that?" asked Eric, interested in anything to do with sports.

"Well, the Chinese don't have much idea about group sports," Dr. Hart explained, "so they had no idea whatsoever about sportsmanship. If one team knew it did not have a chance of winning against the other team, it would refuse to play. If there were a few drops of rain, the boys would run for cover as if they were about to melt, or if one player got hurt accidentally, his whole team would take it personally and walk off the field. The referees had a terrible job trying to get either side to obey the rules, and to top it all off, the boys would not wear sports gear."

"What did they wear?" asked Eric.

"Just what they wore everywhere else, their blue robes. The robes came down to the ground, and the boys were forever tripping over them."

"Do they still dress like that?" Eric inquired.

"Unfortunately, they do," replied Dr. Hart. "We still have a long way to go when it comes to sports."

Eric nodded. Dr. Lavington Hart reminded him very much of his old principal at Eltham College. For both of them, how a boy played sports had a lot to do with how he would play the game of life.

Dr. Hart then showed Eric the classroom he would be teaching in. There Eric got some good news and some bad news. The good news was that he would be able to teach all his classes in English, even though all his students would be Chinese. The bad news was that he would also be teaching several English language classes as well as chemistry. English was Eric's least favorite subject, and the thought of teaching Chinese students English grammar and Shakespeare's plays did not thrill him at all. However, he reminded himself he shouldn't worry too much about it. After all, it wasn't even certain whether he would have any students to teach when the new school year started. The strike was still going strong. Eric would just have to wait and see how things worked out.

Chapter 8

The Flying Scotsman

The remainder of the summer vacation sped by, and soon the school year was about to begin. As starting day approached, the reality of his new responsibilities struck Eric. He had always enjoyed being with children, talking to groups of children in school assemblies, playing games of rugby on a Saturday afternoon with neighborhood boys, even having tea with the founder of his fan club. But being a teacher was quite another matter. Eric began to wonder whether he would be able to control a classroom full of boys. He knew the boys' parents were sending their sons to the Anglo-Chinese college to get the best education available in China. Could he give it to them? He hoped so.

On the first morning of school, Eric arrived before the other teachers and had to wait outside until the doors were unlocked. As he waited, other teachers began to arrive. Once they were finally let into the building, Eric nervously waited with the other teachers to see whether any students would ignore the strike and show up for school. Slowly, a trickle of boys began to arrive. A few of them walked to school, but most came in Cadillacs, Rolls Royces, and Daimlers driven by chauffeurs. All of the boys wore the same uniform, a navy blue Chinese robe that hung all the way to the floor. Eric smiled when he thought of the boys playing tennis or soccer in such an outfit. Finally, by 9:00 A.M. one hundred fifty students had shown up. Even though it was well short of the four hundred boys regularly enrolled, Dr. Hart rang the bell, and the teachers and students filed into the chapel for devotions.

It all reminded Eric of his days at Eltham College. The teachers sat in the front rows, while the boys sat in rows behind them according to class level. First they sang two hymns, and then Dr. Hart gave a short talk from the Bible. For many of the new boys, it was the first time they had heard anything about Christianity. The boys listened politely. The talk was followed by two more hymns, and then the service was over.

After the service, Eric was introduced to a group of twenty boys for whom he would be "house-father." This meant that he would be the teacher they came to if they had problems inside or outside of school. The same group of boys would stay with him for the four years they were at the school.

Over the next week, most of the other striking students returned to school, and things got back to "normal." With the return of all the students, the group of boys to whom Eric was housefather grew from twenty to thirty-eight.

Eric soon discovered that his fears about teaching had been unfounded. It was easy for him to control and teach his classes. Indeed, he looked forward to each day at school. He quickly became the most popular speaker at the morning chapel service. Many of his talks were based upon things the boys did or saw every day at school.

Just as in Scotland, Eric had the knack for making his talks simple yet interesting. One day, for example, Eric explained the origins of the English word *sincere.* He told the boys that it was made up of two words, "sine," meaning without, and "cere," meaning wax. He explained that in the past when a sculptor made a statue, he would sign the bottom of it and add the phrase "Sine cere." In doing so, he was guaranteeing that the work he did on the sculpture had no mistakes that had been covered over with wax to disguise them. Eric told the boys that living the Christian life meant that they did not cover up their character weaknesses and mistakes but instead lived sincere lives. This message must have impressed at least one of the students, because years later, when Eric was in Scotland on furlough, one of his former students wrote him a letter that ended with the words, "Yours without wax."

Eric began a weekly after-school Bible study for the boys he was housefather to. Instead of having them meet at school, he invited all the boys back to the Liddell house so that they could get to know his family and enjoy the special snacks his mother made for them. While only three of the boys in his group came from Christian homes, seventeen signed up to attend the Bible study group. (Some boys lived too far away to attend the group after school.)

In the privacy of Eric's study, which was in the attic room next to his bedroom, many of the boys began to ask serious questions about Christianity. When word finally got around the school that Eric was an Olympic gold medalist, the boys began asking even more questions. Why would a person who had so much "honor" at home come to a foreign country to teach chemistry?

After several months of Bible study, some of the boys came to Eric and asked if they could be baptized. When Eric had satisfied himself that they knew what they were doing, he visited each of their parents to explain the situation. Eric had expected them to be angry that their sons would want to join the Christian religion. Instead, their responses surprised him. At each home, Eric heard the same answer. The parents told Eric that their sons were so much happier and better behaved since they had been going to his Bible study that they wanted them to become Christians. Eric arranged with a local church to hold a baptismal service.

If Eric's Bible study group was going very well, his athletic training at school was not. In fact, he was very frustrated with the boys when it came to sports. He announced one day that he would start teaching them how to play rugby during P.E., but it turned out to be a disaster. Eric dressed in his normal sports gear, white shorts and a tee shirt. But when he walked out onto the sports field, the boys all burst out laughing. They had never seen a white man's knees before! Eric groaned. It seemed ridiculous to even attempt teaching rugby to a group of boys all dressed in robes, but he had little choice.

Things didn't go well from the start. The boys complained bitterly, and privately Eric had to agree with them. The ground they played on was open, and the wind seemed to howl across it, whipping the fine sandy topsoil up into the eyes and mouths of the boys. When the wind was blowing, everyone was soon covered from head to toe with gray dirt. And not only was it windy on the field, but it was also usually either too hot or too cold to play. Tientsin had a difference of more than 100 degrees Fahrenheit between summer and winter temperatures. Even Eric found it too cold to enjoy being outside sometimes.

As for the techniques of rugby, the tackling, the scrum, and rucking the ball, they were nearly impossible to perform in a robe. The boys were constantly tripping over their own or each other's robes. In the scrums and rucks, they would grab the robe of the player next to them and would not let go. The robe would rip, and an embarrassed boy would scurry off the field, vowing never to play rugby again.

Eventually, after more than a year of trying, Eric did manage to convince the boys to wear baggy shorts like his and a shirt. But this had its problems, too. Now the boys didn't have a robe between them and the hard ground when they were tackled or fell. There were many skinned knees and elbows, and the boys could see no point whatsoever in going through so much misery to get a ball from one end of the field to the other. But Eric did not give up on his students—or sports. He, like Dr. Hart, believed that boys could learn a lot about life from sports. However, he did wish there were a few people around who liked playing sports as much as he did.

Fortunately, Tientsin was a very international city. After the Opium Wars, many foreign countries had demanded their own piece of land in China. Such land was known as a concession. Eric lived in the French concession, but there were many other concessions in the city. In fact, thirty countries, most of them from Europe, had concessions in Tientsin. Each concession was guarded by troops from its home country, and inside its walls, the customs and laws of that country were observed. The concessions were southeast of the old Chinese section of Tientsin, and Chinese people were allowed into them only with an invitation and proper identification.

Because of the concessions, Tientsin was a fascinating place to explore. The British, French, and

Japanese concessions were located on the right bank of the Haiho River, and across the river from them were the Russian, Belgian, and Italian concessions. The buildings in each concession were modeled after the architectural style of the particular country that controlled it. A person walking in Tientsin could find himself walking along Victoria Park Road and thinking he was in England, the Rue du Baron Gros thinking he was in France, or the Via Vittorio Emanuele thinking he was in Italy.

Fortunately for Eric, the troops who watched over their particular country's concession liked playing sports with their counterparts from the other concessions. Eric joined the British rugby team and quickly became the fastest wing ever to play rugby on Chinese soil. Playing rugby again brought Eric a great deal of personal satisfaction.

As for his students, Eric felt that they might enjoy sports more if they had a better field to play on. He asked around to find out whether there was a stadium somewhere in Tientsin, perhaps at one of the three universities located in the city or at another boys' high school, where he could take his students to play sports, but there was none. After discussing the situation with Dr. Hart, Eric was given permission to organize for a stadium to be built. He soon formed a committee and found a large tract of unused land near the river. He began to draw up plans. He'd always liked the Stamford Bridge stadium in London, and so he used that as his model. When the stadium was finished, it was by far the best sports stadium in North China, and probably in the whole of Asia. Eric was proud of it and excited to be one of the first to compete in it.

In 1927, the annual International Athletic Games were the first event to be held in the new stadium. Eric was competing in them, and for the first time in his life, his entire family was there to see him run. His brother Robert made the long journey by motorcycle from his mission station in the country to Tientsin to see Eric race.

The day Eric was to run was hot, much like the day three years before in Paris when he had won his gold medal. Along with his family, many of Eric's friends and fellow students were there to watch him compete, as were reporters and photographers from all of Tientsin's seven major newspapers. The photographers were all looking to take that special shot of Eric running that would make the front page of the next day's newspaper. One photographer was so eager to get his shot that once the race had started, he rushed out onto the track to photograph the runners as they came down the home stretch. The crowd could see what was about to happen, but not the photographer—or Eric. Eric was in the lead, and with his head thrust back in his unusual running style, he had no way of seeing the photographer in front of him. Meanwhile, the photographer had no idea just how fast Eric was running. As the photographer was adjusting his camera lens for his "perfect" shot, bang! Eric ran right into him. The photographer flew in one direction, his tripod and camera in another.

After the collision, Eric was sprawled out on the track unconscious. Robert rushed from his seat to help his brother. Finally, Eric came to and managed to stagger off the track. As he did so, he grinned and waved at the photographer. Eric had already forgiven the man for costing him his first win at the new stadium.

The following year another athletic competition was held, right after the 1928 Olympic Games in Amsterdam, Holland. Although Eric could still run like the wind, he had not been invited to be on the British team for those Olympics. He never quite understood why he had not been invited to join the team, but he supposed that most people had thought that since he was in China, he was no longer interested in running.

Whatever the reason, Eric used his participation in the 1928 South Manchurian Games to show that he was still a world-class athlete. He ran the 200-meter race in 21.8 seconds and the 400 meters in 47.8 seconds. Both of these times were faster than the gold medal-winning times at the Amsterdam Olympics. However, one of the most memorable races of Eric's life occurred after the official races were over.

Eric had only thirty minutes between the end of the 400-meter race and the time the boat from Manchuria back to Tientsin would depart. He came up with a plan. Fifteen minutes before the race was to start, he called a taxi and loaded his bags into it. Then he asked the taxi driver to wait near the finish line so that as soon as the race was over, he could continue running right into the taxi and zoom off to the dock the boat would be leaving from. If all went well, Eric could just make it.

Eric easily won the race, but there was one thing he had not taken into account. As soon as he passed the finish line, a band struck up "God Save the King" in his honor. Of course, Eric had no choice but to stop dead in his tracks and stand at attention while the British national anthem was being played. As the last notes faded from the band's instruments, Eric sprinted off towards the taxi. He had nearly reached it when he heard the band begin to play another song. This time it was the French national anthem, the "Marseillaise." A Frenchman had finished second in the race, and now he was being honored. Once again, Eric stood still. It would have been rude to have done anything else. As he stood there only a few feet from the taxi, he wished the band would play faster, but the seconds dragged on.

Finally, Eric made it to the taxi, which began to weave its way as fast as it could through the crowd as it headed for the dock. As the taxi eventually screeched to a halt at the dock, Eric's heart sank. The boat had already cast off and was a good fifteen feet from the pier. Eric clambered from the taxi anyway and ran to the edge of the dock, hoping the captain might see him and turn the boat around. But no one on the boat recognized him. Suddenly, though, a large wave pushed the boat several feet closer to the pier. Eric saw his chance. He hurled his bags onto the boat; then he took a running leap. He sailed through the air and landed flat on his back on the deck of the boat. Startled passengers gathered around him, wanting to know who he was and whether he was all right. A newspaper reporter who saw Eric's leap hurried off to write a story about it. The next morning the headlines read, "Flying Scotsman Leaps Fifteen Feet." Eric Liddell, now had a new nickname, the Flying Scotsman, which would stick with him for the rest of his life.

The story beneath the headline in the newspaper went on to tell about the races that Eric had won at the South Manchurian Games. It was obvious, the paper pointed out, that the world's best quarter-mile runner had not been in Amsterdam competing for a gold medal, but had been in Tientsin working with Chinese boys.

Chapter 9

There Was Just One Problem

"It seems we Liddells are always saying good-bye to each other," Eric commented grimly to his brother Robert.

Robert nodded. "It certainly does. Still, Dad has worked very hard, and I've been a bit worried about his health lately. It's probably a good thing they're taking a two-year furlough."

Eric smiled. He tried to think of it as a good thing, but it was more difficult for him than Robert. Robert had a family of his own now, a wife and a baby girl. Eric, on the other hand, still lived with his parents and loved their company and that of his younger sister and brother. He would miss having them around to talk to. All the time he'd been at school in England he hadn't felt like he knew his family well. He had made a start getting to know them better when they were together in Edinburgh. But since being in China, he felt he'd gotten to know his family on a whole different level. As a result, it was much harder this time to say goodbye to them.

Eric and Robert stood on the dock and watched as their parents, along with Jenny and Ernest, climbed the gangway and boarded the German liner, *Saarbracken*. They waved furiously as the ship pulled away from the dock. As the *Saarbracken* steamed towards the horizon, Eric held onto the one thought that made him happy at that moment. In another year, he, too, would be going back to Scotland on furlough. There, he would stay with his parents in Edinburgh.

With most of his family back in Scotland, Eric had to move out of number 6 London Mission Street, where the family had lived for the past four years. He moved into a four-bedroom apartment in which three other teachers from the Anglo-Chinese college already lived. The apartment had a large living area, and the four roommates had a Chinese servant, Kwei-Lin, who did their shopping, cleaning, and cooking. One of Eric's new roommates was always doing interesting things, and Eric learned a lot from him. Another roommate had a large stamp collection, and Eric soon started a collection of his own. Eric's third roommate played billiards and taught Eric how to play. He probably regretted it, because Eric was a fast learner. Soon Eric could beat him, and just about anyone else in Tientsin who played billiards. When Eric was not busy with stamp collecting, billiards, or his sports and teaching responsibilities at school, he served as Sunday school superintendent for the Union Church.

Despite being so busy, Eric felt lonely without his parents around. He was twenty-seven, and for the first time in his life he began to think seriously about getting married and having children of his own. He had no idea whom he would marry, but slowly he began to notice one particular young woman, Florence McKenzie, or Flo, as everyone called her. Flo had been staying at Pei-tia-ho with her parents when Eric first arrived in China. She was petite, with sparkly brown eyes and long, curly black hair. She played the organ at church, was a strong Christian, and loved to laugh and play practical jokes. Eric loved being around her.

There was just one problem. Florence McKenzie was only seventeen years old and in her last year of high school. Eric had to come up with some way to get to know her better without making it look like he was dating someone ten years his junior. After giving it much thought, he decided to befriend the entire graduating class at Tientsin Grammar School. He would invite all the students to the popular Kiesslings Cafe for afternoon tea or take them on a walk or a picnic. On these outings, he would spend time with Flo. Of course, he tried to make it look as though he was just being friendly with her, as he was with the other students. But the more time he spent around her, the more he liked her.

Finally, Eric decided that she was the one he wanted to marry. Trouble was, he was too shy to ask her. He worried that she might say no, or worse, that she'd say yes while her parents said no. He wasn't sure what to do, so he just kept taking the entire graduating class out for cups of tea at Kiesslings Cafe.

Eventually, summer vacation rolled around, and Eric, along with his roommates, went to stay at Pei-tai-ho. Understandably, Eric was thrilled to learn that the McKenzie family, including Flo, would also be staying there for the summer, and in a cabin only two doors down from his. Eric became the chief organizer of outings for the summer. He arranged a four-day walking tour up nearby Mount Pei-niu-ting, tennis tournaments, picnics by the sea, play readings, anything that brought him and Flo together. His three roommates soon began to notice that whatever event Eric planned, he always made sure Flo knew about it.

On these outings, Eric learned a lot more about Flo. Flo told him she was going back to Toronto (where her family was from) in the fall to train as a nurse. The training would take four years. After training, when she was twenty-one, Flo planned to return to China to work in a hospital. Eric's heart raced as he thought about it. He knew he couldn't marry a seventeen-year-old, but what about a twenty-one-year-old? That would be a perfect age for a woman to get married.

Eric waited until he returned to Tientsin to ask Flo to marry him. At first she thought he was joking.

After all, Eric Liddell was a famous Olympic champion, and she was just a young woman fresh out of high school. "Are you sure you really mean this?" she asked him.

"Yes, I do," he replied simply.

Flo didn't have to think hard about her answer. Eric's proposal was a dream come true, and Flo eagerly accepted. Flo's parents cheerfully gave their permission for the couple to eventually marry. Soon Eric was writing home to his mother, asking her to buy an engagement ring with five diamonds and send it to him in China. The ring arrived just before Flo and her family were to return to Toronto. Eric presented the ring to Flo, and so began their four-year engagement. The couple planned to marry when Flo finished nursing school.

After Flo left China, Eric began to prepare for a yearlong furlough in Scotland. As always, he had lots of plans. He decided he would use the year to study to become an ordained minister in the Scottish Congregational church. Along with teaching, this would allow him to do more "traditional" missionary work, such as running a church and baptizing new converts. He also planned to make time in his travels to visit Flo both on his way home from China and on his trip back to China. What he didn't plan for, though, was the fact that he wasn't the only person making plans for his stay in Scotland. It had been seven years since Eric had won his gold medal, and since there had been another Olympic Games in that time, Eric assumed that everyone in Scotland had forgotten him. He assumed wrong.

After a wonderful visit with Flo in Canada, which ended all too soon, Eric was back on a ship headed across the Atlantic Ocean for the British Isles. When he finally arrived in Edinburgh, his welcome was a huge surprise. Instead of being forgotten, Eric Liddell was more popular than ever. A large Welcome Home gathering, organized by a number of well-known Scottish ministers and sports stars, was held for him. Eric was stunned. All over the country, people wanted him to speak at or attend dinners in his honor.

These engagements quickly mounted up until Eric could hardly keep track of all the invitations he received. He hated to think that he might forget one by mistake, because he didn't want to disappoint anyone. After a few weeks, the college at which he was studying to become an ordained minister set up an Eric Liddell committee to handle Eric's appointments. This was a great relief to Eric, as it gave him more time during the week to study. On the weekends he spoke wherever the committee had arranged for him to be. He still got nervous when he spoke in public at these events, but he realized he had a wonderful opportunity to tell people about missionary work and the needs of China.

These events weren't confined to Scotland. Eric traveled to England and Ireland to speak. Everywhere he went, the Flying Scotsman received a hero's welcome, and many people who otherwise never went to church listened eagerly to his talks.

Eric was delighted to be back in Edinburgh living with his family. He spent time with many of his friends, too. D. P. Thomson, who had arranged Eric's first talk in Armadale six years before, traveled to many of the meetings with Eric. Eric also visited Elsa McKechnie and her family. Elsa was still the head of his official fan club. She and Eric had written regularly to each other during the years he'd been in China, and she was delighted to see him again in person. Although Eric had two or three meetings to speak at every weekend during his furlough, he felt most comfortable when talking to people like Elsa one-on-one. When he looked out at a huge audience, he would try to think of them as individuals and not just one large group.

Eric always had a real concern for each person he met, and it was this attitude that made him different from many other famous people. On one occasion, Eric was visiting a large church. While there, the pastor asked him to sign the visitors' book. Eric was happy to do so, and when he had finished signing his name, he wrote a Chinese character beside it.

"What does that mean?" asked the pastor.

"It's Chinese for 'keep smiling,'" replied Eric.

The pastor smiled. "How nice. I will be sure to show it to one of the women in my church. She always signs her letters and notes with those words—in English, of course."

Eric nodded.

"Sometimes it doesn't seem she has a lot to smile about," continued the pastor. "She was in a bad accident five years ago, and she has been in and out of the hospital ever since."

"What's the matter with her?" asked Eric.

"Just about everything. Her scalp was torn off, and she lost one eye in the accident. The doctors were able to do skin grafts on her, but it has all been so very painful. She's nearly blind and deaf and gets terrible headaches. But she will love to see 'keep smiling' in the visitors' book. That's her message to us all."

"Would she have time for a visit from me?" inquired Eric.

The pastor looked surprised. "You would visit her? I can't think of anything she would love more than a visit from you!"

And so it was that Eric visited Bella Montgomery in her small brick terrace home. The two of them spent an hour together, happily chatting away. Eric marveled at her wonderful attitude. After he'd left, Bella Montgomery wrote a letter thanking him for his visit. The letter arrived in the mail just as Eric was about to catch a train for London for a speaking engagement. Eric stuffed the letter into his jacket pocket so that he could read it on the train when he had more time.

Once on the train, Eric found himself alone in a compartment. When he had stowed his bags in the overhead rack, he sat down to read Bella Montgomery's letter. He smiled as he read. The grammar and spelling were not perfect, but the letter told of how Bella had found Jesus Christ to be her best friend through all her problems. When he had finished reading, Eric folded the letter neatly and tucked it back in his jacket pocket.

At the next station, a young man boarded the train and seated himself in the same compartment with Eric. From the look on the man's face, Eric could see that he was very unhappy. As the train chugged through the countryside, the young man's story came out. He had lost his job, his girlfriend had left him, and his family had branded him a complete failure. He told Eric he could see no reason to go on living and wondered whether suicide might be the answer to how he was feeling.

At first Eric couldn't think of the right words to say to the young man, but then he realized he didn't have to. He slid his hand into his jacket pocket and pulled out Bella Montgomery's letter. "Here, read this," he said as he handed it to the man.

"It's no use," the young man replied, placing his head in his hands.

"Please, read it. It's only a page."

Eric's voice soothed the man, who reached out and took the letter. When the man had finished reading, Eric told him a little about Bella Montgomery and how she was able to see difficult circumstances as opportunities. By the time the train arrived in London, the young man was much happier than he had been. Bella Montgomery's letter had inspired him. He was no longer talking about suicide but was considering the possibilities he would find in London.

While home on furlough, Eric had decided not to do any running, since there wasn't enough time to fit it in. Eric made one exception, though. While in London, he visited his old school, Eltham College.

All the boys who attended the school knew about its most famous "old boy." The walls in the administration building were all lined with many athletic plaques and trophies that Eric and his brother had won for the school. Eric had been invited to Eltham College to present the prizes at the annual sports day. He was glad for the opportunity to do so, but it was not enough for the boys, who wanted to see Eric Liddell run on his "home track." Finally, after a lot of good-natured nagging, Eric agreed to race in the 220 yards against the best runners in the school. He strolled up to the starting line in his regular shoes, his jacket draped casually over his arm, and not looking at all like a serious runner. When the starter's pistol fired, though, it was another story. Eric shot off his mark and streaked around the track, finishing a long way in front of the best runner in the school. The students whistled and clapped for the champion who had once been just like them.

Wherever he went around the British Isles, people asked Eric what he thought about the political situation in China. Was there going to be a war? Who did he think would win it? These were difficult questions. Scotland was a long way from Tientsin, and circumstances were changing so rapidly in China that sometimes Eric didn't know what to make of it all. The Nationalist army, under General Chiang Kai-shek, and the Communist forces were engaged in many vicious clashes with each other across the country, especially in north-central China.

Villages were burned, homes were looted, and crops were destroyed wherever there was fighting.

In 1931, Japan, realizing that China was in a weakened state, invaded Manchuria in the north. At first, Eric's friends from the Anglo-Chinese college had written and told him that there was not much fighting around Tientsin and that life was going on as normal. Then about two-thirds of the way through his furlough, Eric began to get letters from China that confirmed what he'd read in the newspapers. The Japanese had become bolder. They had bombed Shanghai, the busiest port in China. Japanese gunboats and aircraft had flattened large tracts of the city with their relentless bombing. Eventually, Britain had been able to get Japan to stop the attack, but the future for China did not look stable. The country was in a three-way tug of war between the Communists, the Nationalists, and the Japanese, and Eric had no idea who would finally win. All the questions, though, made him want to get back to China more than ever. There was a lot of missionary work still to be done there!

Towards the end of his furlough, there was a lot of excitement in the Liddell home. Jenny was getting married to Dr. Charles Somerville, and Eric was able to attend the ceremony, as were Robert and his family, who had just arrived home on furlough. The whole family was together again, which made the wedding a wonderful occasion.

Another wonderful family event took place in June 1932, when Eric passed his exams and was ordained as a minister in the Scottish Congregational church. He was now the Reverend Eric Liddell. With his ordination, however, it was time for him to return to China. Of course, he hated leaving his parents again, especially since his father had been given some difficult news. Eric's parents would not be returning to China as they had planned. The London Missionary Society had decided that James Liddell was not in very good health and it was time for him to retire from missionary work. As Eric made preparations for his return, he comforted himself with the thought that in some way, at least, he would be able to take his father's place in China.

Eric was both sorry and excited as he set out for China again. Saying good-bye to his family was hard, but on the other hand, he had a visit in Toronto to look forward to.

Chapter 10

Together at Last

Eric spent six weeks with Flo and her family in Toronto. The time went by far too quickly, but Eric was able to tell Flo all about Jenny's wedding, and together they made some early preparations for their own in wedding in Tientsin. They decided to be married in March 1934, right after Flo returned to China at the completion of her nursing training.

By September 1932, Eric was back in Tientsin ready for the start of a new school year. All of his old responsibilities were waiting for him. Eric was once again housefather to a group of boys and Sunday school superintendent at Union Church. He also took on some new responsibilities. He was made secretary of the Anglo-Chinese college and chairman of the sports committee. And now that he was an ordained minister, he took on more speaking engagements in churches. He also wrote long letters home to his parents once a week. Since his parents were no longer returning to China, they wanted to know all about what he was doing and whether he had seen any of their old friends. On top of all this, Eric was still a schoolteacher, with lessons to plan and papers to grade. But Eric liked all the extra work; it helped him pass the time while he waited for Flo to return.

Everything went well for Eric until November 1933, when he received a telegram telling him that his father had died suddenly the day before. Eric felt sad and helpless. He and Robert were both on the other side of the world at a time when their mother needed them most, with no way to make it home in time for the funeral. With the news of James Liddell's death, many people, both missionaries and Chinese nationals, came to comfort Eric. Eric's father had made an impact on a great many lives in and around Tientsin, and Eric renewed his determination to do the same.

During the next few weeks, Eric thought often about Jenny's wedding. No one had suspected it then, but it was the last time the Liddells would be together as a family. Still, if he and Robert couldn't be with their mother, Eric was comforted by the fact that Jenny and Ernest were there to help her. In one letter to his mother, shortly after James Liddell's death, Eric wrote, "Jenny's garden will soon be in bloom again. You must go there, Mother, and stay with her, especially at this time of year. I am glad that I recently had a furlough and was with you, for now I can picture it all so clearly and see what you are doing."

If word of his father's death saddened and depressed Eric, the news that Flo and her mother were aboard the *Empress of Canada* bound for Taku, China, lifted his spirits. Eric could hardly wait for Flo to arrive. Finally, he and Flo would be together. The ship was making stops in Hawaii and Japan and was due to dock in China on or about March 1, 1934. Flo wrote and told Eric that she would cable him from Japan with the exact date that the ship would arrive in Taku.

Eric had a lot to do. His three roommates had all left to work in other places, leaving Eric alone in the apartment. The Anglo-Chinese college, which owned the place, gave permission for Eric and Flo to make it their home after they were married. Eric set about transforming the apartment into a suitable home for a married couple. The walls were repainted. New furniture was bought or borrowed, and the kitchen was scrubbed down. Finally, everything was ready, and all Eric could do was wait. Although it had been only eighteen months since he had last seen Flo, it seemed like forever.

Eventually, the day of Flo's arrival in Taku rolled around. Her father had returned to China a few months earlier, and together he and Eric made the hour-long train trip from Tientsin to Taku. But when they arrived, bad news awaited them. The ship had been delayed by rough weather in the Yellow Sea.

The two men spent the night at a friend's house in Taku, and the next day, made their way to the dock to meet the ship. Again, they were met by bad news. Gale-force winds were still whipping up the sea, and through the haze of sea spray, Eric could see the *Empress of Canada* out towards the horizon. The ship was being tossed and turned by mountainous waves that beat against its hull. Although the ship was so close, the harbormaster informed them of the latest delay. The *Empress of Canada* needed fifteen feet of water clearance to safely enter the harbor and dock. But the tide was on the way out, and with such dangerous winds, the ship dare not try to enter the harbor. Instead, it would wait for the wind to drop or for the next high tide.

Dejected, Eric and Mr. McKenzie made the trek back to their friend's home. No sooner had they arrived there than news came that the ship was being battered so fiercely by the wind and the waves that the captain had decided to risk docking it during the storm.

By the time they got back to the harbor, the *Empress of Canada* was pulling parallel to the dock. Tugboats had begun to maneuver the ship closer, when a huge gust of wind caught the ship and spun its stern towards the dock. Onlookers gasped and shut their eyes, waiting for the sound of tearing metal as the dock and the ship collided. Fortunately, that did not happen. The tugs frantically pulled on the stern lines, and slowly the ship straightened. Finally, longshoremen scrambled for the ropes thrown from the *Empress of Canada.* They placed them over the bollards that lined the edge of the dock, and soon the ship was tied up securely. A gangway was swung into place, and Eric waited anxiously for Flo to walk down it.

Finally, Eric spotted Flo. He grinned broadly and hurried to the end of the gangway to greet her. Once they were together, it was hard to know what to talk about first—Flo's exams, the voyage from Canada, the trip Flo had made to Scotland several months earlier to visit Eric's mother, or the colors Eric had chosen for the walls of their new home. All the topics merged, one into another, and the two of them talked until five the next morning, when it was time to catch the train back to Tientsin.

Three weeks later, on March 27, 1934, Florence McKenzie and Eric Liddell were married at Union Church in Tientsin. The popular couple's wedding drew a huge crowd. Indeed, a report of the ceremony was carried on the front page of newspapers in both Tientsin and Peking. The newlyweds took a brief honeymoon in Peiping, a few miles to the west of Tientsin, before returning to settle in Eric's apartment.

Flo had a great time arranging everything. She pulled all Eric's trophies and medals from the boxes he'd stuffed them in years before. She insisted on hanging them on the walls or displaying them on the mantelpiece. At first, Eric found it difficult to get used to seeing all his trophies out where others could see them. He was concerned that people might think he was showing off. But he could see that Flo was proud of them, so he let her have her way.

Inside Eric and Flo's new home there was lots of laughter and fun. Outside, though, the storm clouds of war were continuing to gather. No one knew just what would happen, but everyone agreed that things could not continue as they had in the past. England's "golden" days in China were drawing to a close. China wanted to take control of her own destiny. The big question to be answered was, What was her destiny? Would it be a China controlled by a nationalist government or a government controlled by the Communists, who continued to gain power in the countryside? And what about the Japanese? Neither the Communists nor the Nationalists seemed to be able to stop fighting each other long enough to repel the Japanese invaders.

The local government in Tientsin began to prepare for war. It ordered all boys' schools in the city to conduct military training for their students. Eric was not at all happy about this. It was hard to think of a Christian school teaching boys how to kill and maim others, but the school had no choice but to follow the local government's orders. Something good came out of it, though. All the training for war made many of the boys at the Anglo-Chinese college think more seriously about their religious beliefs. Soon new Bible study groups were springing up all over campus. Still, it was a sober time that reminded Eric of how life had been at Eltham College back in London as the older boys had prepared to go off and fight in the First World War.

Despite the tension and uncertainty over what lay ahead for China, the first year of marriage passed quickly for Eric and Flo. It also produced a new member of their family, baby Patricia. A year later, Patricia got a sister, Heather. Flo enjoyed telling the story of how Heather came to get her name. Being Scottish, Eric had wanted to name his new daughter Heather, after the purple flowering shrubs that grew on the hillsides of Scotland. Flo wasn't so enthusiastic; she had another name in mind for the new baby. Eric offered to solve the matter by writing both names on slips of paper and drawing one out of a hat. The two of them agreed to name the baby whichever name was drawn. With great flourish, Eric folded the two slips of paper and put them into a hat. He held the hat up for Flo to select one. When she unfolded the slip of paper it read, "Heather." Flo stuck to the agreement and announced that the baby would be called Heather. Finally, Eric burst out laughing. He dipped his hand into the hat and pulled out the other piece of paper. It had Heather written on it, too! Flo laughed with him. If Eric wanted that badly to have his second daughter named Heather, he could have his way.

The summer of 1936 should have been happy and carefree for the Liddells, but it turned out to be a time of serious consideration about their future in China. Flo and the girls went off to the beach town of Pei-tia-ho to escape the heat of Tientsin. In August, Eric was to join them for several weeks' vacation. However, in July, Eric was asked to meet with the board of directors of the District Council of the London Missionary Society, which financially supported him and his new family. At the meeting, the directors told Eric about the very difficult situation they were in. It was a matter of distribution, they said. Too many of their missionaries were in the cities, where life was going on fairly normally, and too few were in the countryside, where there was terrible destruction from the ongoing fighting. The London Missionary Society leaders in England were putting pressure on the local board of directors to take some of the teachers from Tientsin and send them to one of the hardest hit areas, Siao Chang.

Eric nodded silently as he listened to what was being said.

"Of course, your name was one of the first to come up," said the board chairman. "We know you spent some of your childhood in Siao Chang, and your brother Robert is a doctor in our hospital there. Being an ordained minister, you would be a perfect choice to be village evangelist there."

"But there is one thing that makes this difficult," said another board member. "The plains are no place for a wife and small children. The conditions there are terrible. There is fighting everywhere, and no one can keep up with who is winning or whose side anyone is on. It's a complete mess. The peasants and farmers have given up on the Nationalists and think the Communists might be able to help them more. The warlords are fighting hard to keep their control over the peasants. And while everyone is fighting among themselves, the Japanese are silently and efficiently moving south."

"Yes, Siao Chang is no place for a woman and small children," echoed the board chairman.

"Aye. I hear it has become quite desperate in Siao Chang," agreed Eric. "My brother tells me in his letters some of what is going on. Last week he wrote about the babies who have been brought to the hospital because their mothers have been killed in the fighting. He said the nurses were trying to save the babies' lives with soybean products, but most of the babies died without their mother's milk."

"Then you know what you'll be up against," said another board member. "All in all, we think you would be the best person to send there. Unfortunately, as we pointed out, it's no place for your wife or children. You would have to leave them in Tientsin and come back for regular visits."

Eric sat quietly. For several weeks there had been talk in the staff room at the Anglo-Chinese college that something like this might happen. Eric had thought they might ask him to go, even though he'd been on staff at the college for ten years now. He never expected, however, that it would mean being separated from his new family. He didn't know what to say.

As the meeting drew to a close, the board chairman cleared his throat and spoke. "Anyway, it's not something you have to decide right away. We wouldn't send you until the end of the next school year. Talk to your wife about it, and we'll call you in to hear what you have to say in October."

"Thank you," replied Eric. "This is not a decision I can make lightly. I'll pray about it and talk to my wife."

As the train chugged closer to Pei-tia-ho, Eric was still thinking about the meeting. He wondered how to tell Flo what the District Council had asked him to do. And, more important, he wondered whether it was the right thing for him to do. He was going to have to do a lot of serious thinking and praying during his summer vacation.

Chapter 11

Li Mu Shi

Eric Liddell finally made up his mind. He would go to Siao Chang to work among the peasants and farmers who had been stripped of all hope by the constant fighting going on around them. Many of Eric's teacher friends at the Anglo-Chinese college thought Eric had been pressured into making the decision by the mission's board of directors, but Flo knew better. She remembered Eric's telling her the story of how he had refused to run on Sunday at the Olympic Games. Even though all Scotland had seemed to be against him and his decision not to run, Eric had stuck to his decision. Eric was soft-spoken and still a little shy, but there was no way other people's opinions could cause him to do something he didn't think was right or stop him from doing something he felt God had called him to.

In late December 1937, Eric loaded his luggage onto a riverboat. The time for him to leave had come. With a heavy heart, Eric hugged Flo and his two daughters, Patricia and Heather, good-bye and climbed aboard the boat that would take him on the ten-day journey inland to Siao Chang. He stood at the stern of the riverboat and waved until the three people he loved most in the world became a blur at the river's edge.

The London Missionary Society compound in Siao Chang was much the same as it had been when Eric lived there as small boy with his parents. Eric was five years old when he left, and surprisingly, he remembered much about the place and his life there. When he saw the thick wall that enclosed the compound, he remembered walking around the top of it, looking out at the endless countryside beyond the village. He remembered the house the family had lived in and the field beside it where his parents had allowed the children to keep goats. The sign reading "Chung Wia I Chai" (Chinese and Foreigners, all One Home) still hung over the gates to the compound. It was faded now. It had been hung there thirty-five years before when his parents had first arrived. That had been during the turmoil of the Boxer Rebellion when many Chinese people blamed all their problems on "foreign devils." The villagers had hung the sign as a way of telling James and Mary Liddell they were welcome in the village. Now, an even greater danger than the Boxer Rebellion was threatening the peace and stability of Siao Chang.

Eric familiarized himself with the parts of the compound that either he did not remember or had been added since he had left. He visited his brother Robert in the hundred-bed hospital where he worked. He also met Dr. Kenneth McAll, who worked with Robert, and was introduced to Annie Buchan, the hospital matron and a fellow Scot.

Many of the people around Siao Chang remembered Eric as a small boy in the village. They told him stories about his father, whom they had called, *Li Mu Shi.* (Li was short for Liddell, and Mu Shi was "pastor" in Chinese.) Now they called Eric by the same name.

The London Missionary Society director for the area met with Eric to explain to him his new duties. It was simple, really, but dangerous. There were over ten thousand villages on the Great Plain, and Siao Chang was the center of missionary activity for all of them. Most of these villages were in a terrible situation. The past six years had been very difficult for the people who lived in the villages. A string of massive droughts had been followed by torrential rains and then widespread flooding. In 1937, as a result of the continual cycle of drought and flood, crop yields were less than half what they normally were. Even without any of the political and military problems in the area, people had been finding it hard to survive over the past few years. The war had just made things more intolerable.

Because there were so many villages, neither the Communists, the Nationalists, nor the Japanese had enough soldiers to occupy them all at one time. As a result, one army, for example, the Communists, would take over a village. The soldiers would eat all the food they could find, drag many men off to join their army, kill those who resisted, assault the women, and burn down the houses of anyone they suspected of being a Nationalist or Japanese sympathizer. After several weeks, they would get bored and decide to take over another village. The Communists would then move out, and the Nationalists would move in and do the same things to the village and its people. Eventually, they would move on, and the Japanese army would move in. It was a depressing cycle for those who lived in the villages because they had little power to stop what was happening to them.

Eric's job was to visit the villages across the plain, encourage the Christian villagers, and hold evangelistic meetings for those who had not yet heard the gospel message. It sounded like a simple enough task, but it was not. The Communists in particular hated Christianity, and a missionary was likely to be shot on the spot. To make it a little safer for Eric, the Red Cross gave him an armband to wear and listed his official title as "Hospital Accountant" rather than missionary. Not only was Eric's new job dangerous, it was also depressing. No one could crisscross the huge plains without seeing horrible sights. Sometimes Eric could do something to help those he encountered. Sadly though, it was often too late for him to be of any help.

Eric wasted no time getting started in his new job. Because there were so many different dialects spoken across the Great Plain, he took an interpreter, Wang Feng Chou, with him on his travels. The first thing Eric did before they set out was teach Wang Feng to ride a bicycle so that the two of them could get around more quickly than they could walking. Poor Wang Feng did not have nice smooth roads to learn to ride on but encountered potholed tracks that had been bombed over and over. Because of the condition of the roads, at least once a day both Wang and Eric were pitched off their bikes onto the hard ground by potholes. At the end of a trip, Eric's body was often covered with bruises from all the spills off his bike.

Sometimes Eric and Wang Feng were able to ride to a nearby village, preach, visit the Christians there, and return to Siao Chang all in one day. Other times, they went farther afield and would spend the night wherever they were invited to stay. On these occasions, they normally slept on the dirt floor of a hut and went to bed hungry, just like everyone else in the house. There was usually not enough food for a family to eat, let alone to feed visitors.

The faint flicker of a lamp would light up a small loom at one end of the room. Through the night, family members would take turns weaving cotton thread into fabric. Since the crops had failed so miserably, the only way to make a few pennies was to weave fabric. Thus, it became very important for a family to keep its loom working twenty-four hours a day. The click, click of the loom became a background sound against which the family went about its daily goal of scraping together enough food to survive.

Eric worked closely with the hospital. Since he was always out and about in the countryside, he knew what kinds of injuries people were likely to arrive at the hospital with and from which areas they would be coming. Knowing the kinds of injuries it could expect helped the hospital to respond better to people's needs.

Until the time Eric arrived, the doctors at the hospital had been reluctant to help Japanese or Communist soldiers wounded in the fighting. Although their grip on power was slipping fast, the Nationalists were still recognized as the legitimate government of China, and the hospital didn't want to offend the Nationalist forces by treating soldiers from opposing armies. Besides, both the Japanese and the Communists despised and killed Christians. Slowly, though, Eric's example began to change this reluctance on the part of the doctors. Eric gave help to anyone who needed it, regardless of which side the person was on. Many on the hospital staff asked him how he could help Japanese soldiers when they were killing so many Chinese people. Eric simply pointed out that he saw every human being as someone God loved. His attitude began to spread throughout the hospital, and soon Chinese and Japanese, Communists and Nationalists, found love and help at the London Missionary Society Hospital.

Sometimes Eric would be asked to go and "fetch" a wounded person and bring him or her to the hospital. Often the local people would be too afraid to transport a wounded person because they feared being caught by an opposing army and killed.

On February 19, 1938, the hospital received word that a wounded Communist soldier was lying in a temple in a village about twenty miles from the hospital. Eric was asked to find the wounded man and bring him back to the hospital for treatment. A Chinese man volunteered to go along because he felt nothing bad would happen to him if he traveled with Eric.

The Chinese man set out alone with a cart on which to transport the wounded soldier. Several hours later, Eric caught up to him on his bike. When they reached the village of Pei Lin Tyu, Eric spoke to one of the village elders. "I understand you have an injured soldier here," he said.

"Yes," replied the elder. "He's in the temple. I know it is cold and damp in there, but we could not do anything else. If any of us took him into our home and the Japanese found him there, our whole family would be killed." The elder shrugged his shoulders in frustration at the events that had overtaken his village.

Eric nodded understandingly. "These are difficult times. Please show me where he is."

The village elder led Eric to a small temple and stopped at the bottom of the steps that led up to it.

"He is in there," he said pointing up the steps. "He has received food each day, and someone gave him some straw to sleep on. He has been in there for five days. But with the Japanese only a mile away in the next village, we dare not do more. It would be foolish."

The elder turned and left, and Eric climbed the steps and entered the temple alone. In the dim light inside he could make out a figure lying on a thin pile of straw. The sleeping man had a torn blanket pulled up over him, hardly enough to ward off the subzero winter temperatures. Eric walked over and knelt down beside him. The man awoke. Panic spread across his face. The man shielded his eyes with his hand.

"No, No! Don't kill me," he pleaded.

Eric calmed him down and explained why he was there. Since it was nearly nightfall, much too late to start the trip back, Eric promised the soldier he would return first thing in the morning and transport him to the hospital.

That night, as Eric lay on the cold floor of a Chinese Christian's home, he wondered what he would say if he met any Japanese soldiers the next day. How would he explain transporting a wounded Chinese soldier? Unable to sleep, he opened the Chinese New Testament that he always carried with him. He angled it toward the moonlight that streamed in through the one window in the room and read Luke 16:10: "He that is faithful in that which is least is faithful also in much." Eric felt better. He knew that he was being faithful to God in getting the wounded man to the hospital, and he would trust God to watch over him as he did so.

The next morning, Eric's Chinese companion pulled the cart to the front of the temple. How different it was from the silent place it had been the night before. Now it was bustling with activity. It was Chinese New Year, and all the villagers were dressed in their best clothes, chanting and burning incense in the temple.

Eric rushed up the steps, wondering where the people might have put the wounded soldier while they held their celebration. Was he lying out back in the icy cold wind? Eric didn't have to look far for his answer. The villagers hadn't moved the man at all! The soldier was lying on his pile of straw right where Eric had left him. The temple worshipers just ignored him and moved around him as if he were not there. The air was thick with the smoke from incense, causing Eric to cough. This was no place for a weak and wounded man to be. Quickly, Eric ordered the worshipers and their incense outside. Too surprised to refuse, they all filed out the door. Eric followed them.

The people all stared at the blue-eyed, blond-haired man who had spoken in their dialect and ordered them outside. Eric raised his hand and began to speak. He told them how difficult it was for a sick person to breathe in such a smoke-laden place. Then he recited some Bible verses to them about how God does not want burnt offerings but instead wants people who are just and merciful and who walk humbly with Him. Then he motioned for his traveling companion, and together the two of them went back into the temple and carried out the wounded soldier. They laid the man on the cart and headed for the hospital. Eric rode alongside on his bicycle to make sure the man was comfortable.

When they reached the next village, Huo Chu, two local men ran out to meet them. "Stop! Are you the ones with the wounded man?" they asked.

Eric nodded.

"There is another man here at our village. He is nearly dead. Will you take him to the hospital also?" they pleaded.

Eric climbed from his bike. "What's wrong with him?" he asked.

"It was last week," blurted the taller of the two men who had stopped them. "The Japanese came through the village. They rounded up six men they said were spying against them. One by one they told each man to kneel down, and then they chopped off his head with a sword. The first five obeyed, but the sixth man would not kneel. The Japanese soldier lunged at his neck, slashing it with his sword. The man fell to the ground, and the Japanese thought he was dead. When they left, we found he was still alive, but he had been very badly cut. We hid him in a house, but there is nothing else we can do for him now. Will you help?"

Eric looked at the cart. It was big enough for only one man to lie on. But it seemed unlikely that this other man could wait while Eric took the wounded soldier to the hospital and then came back for him the following day.

"Yes, we will do what we can. Take us to him," he finally said.

For the second time in two days, Eric found himself in a dimly lit room staring at a severely injured man. The man looked to be about forty years old and was rather stout. A dirty bandage encrusted with dried blood was coiled around his neck and the lower half of his face. The man could not talk, but he watched every move Eric made.

Eric unwound the bandage. A deep crimson gash ran from the side of the man's mouth all the way to the back of his neck. Eric gently replaced the bandage. The man obviously needed to get to a hospital, but it wasn't going to be an easy trip for him.

Eric spoke quietly to the wounded man. "We can get you to a hospital. Unfortunately, we have only a small cart. It fits a single man lying down, and we already have a wounded soldier we're transporting. We can take you, but you will have to sit on the shaft of the cart. Do you think you are strong enough to do that?"

The man waved his hand as if to say yes and tried to get up from the bed. Eric hooked his arm under the man's and gently led him outside. It would be a bumpy ride across the bomb-scarred roads, but Eric knew getting to the hospital was the only hope of recovery for both of his passengers.

The normal three-hour trip back to Siao Chang seemed to take forever. Eric and his companion pulling the cart had to constantly stop to adjust the positions of the patients they were transporting. Japanese bombers circled menacingly in the sky only a mile or so away, where they were most likely escorting Japanese troops marching to their next village of victims. Eric knew that the pilots could spot him and his wounded cargo at any time. Their mercy mission went unnoticed, though, and they finally reached the hospital at four in the afternoon, just as the winter sun was beginning to set.

The hospital staff were waiting to operate. Two days later, despite their best efforts, the Communist soldier Eric had retrieved from the temple died. The man with the slashed neck, however, was stitched up and began to make a full recovery. Eric visited the man in the hospital often and discovered that he was an artist. Eric then asked for some paints and paper from one of the nurses, and over the next few weeks the man painted many beautiful pictures of flowers which he insisted on giving to Eric. The paintings were the only thing the man had with which to say thank you to the person who had helped save his life.

While Eric was thankful that the man's life had been saved, he was also a little frustrated. While he had helped save one man's life, everyday across the Great Plain, people were dying from the fighting and the harsh conditions they were forced to endure. Eric wished he could do more. He wished the fighting would stop and everything would get better. However, things would get a lot worse in China before they would get any better.

Chapter 12

More Coal

Slowly the Japanese began to get the upper hand on the Great Plain. They showed some respect for the work of the London Missionary Society hospital, but not a lot. One night, not too long after Eric had rescued the man with the slashed neck, a huge commotion broke out in the men's ward of the hospital. Eric awoke with a start. Hearing the noise, he leapt out of bed, pulled his clothes on over his pajamas, and rushed off to see what was happening. When he reached the ward, he was met by a grim-faced Dr. McAll.

"What's happened?" he asked.

"As far as we can make out, the Communists jumped the hospital compound wall and kidnapped one of the Japanese soldiers we were treating, the one with the bullet wound in his leg," said Dr. McAll.

Eric gave a low whistle. "How long ago?"

"Not more than five minutes. It gave the night nurse a terrible scare. They dragged him off like a sack of rice. I wish they wouldn't use the hospital as a combat zone." Dr. McAll sighed and shook his head as he spoke.

"I wonder what the Japanese will do when they find out one of their men has been captured," Eric mused.

As if to answer his question, a hail of machine-gun bullets hit the hospital wall, and Eric could hear the whistle of mortar bombs. Eric and Dr. McAll looked at each other, their eyes wide with disbelief.

"It's got to be the Japanese," Eric blurted. "They must think the Communists are still inside the hospital compound somewhere."

Dr. McAll turned quickly towards the door. "I'll try to reach them and convince the commander they've made a mistake. You see what you can do for the patients. Move the ones by the windows if you can," he yelled back over his shoulder at Eric.

Much to Eric's relief, ten minutes later, the attack ended as abruptly as it had begun. Several minutes after that, Dr. McAll strolled back into the hospital with a smile on his face. "Everything's all right here, I take it?" he said, looking at Eric.

Eric nodded and then replied, "Yes, but some of the patients are pretty shaken up. How did it go with the commander?"

"Quite extraordinary really. Let's go outside and check up on the damage, and I'll tell you all about it," he said.

When he had shut the door behind them, Dr. McAll told his story. He had been taken to a small hut just outside the compound where a Japanese colonel was lying on a couch.

"At first he would not even turn around to look at me," said the doctor, "so I started talking to him in Chinese, hoping to get his attention. That didn't work, so I started in on pidgin English. He let me go on for a minute or two, and then all at once he jumped off the couch and yelled something in Japanese. The two guards who had brought me to see him hurried out of the room and shut the door behind them. Then the colonel turned to me and said with an American accent, 'Forget it buddy!'

"'So you speak English?' I asked. He nodded and hung his head. He told me his parents were from Japan but he had been born and raised in California. Although he was born in the United States, he decided to help the Japanese win the war in China. He was most unhappy, though. He said, 'Now all I ever do is kill. I don't know how to get out of this mess.'"

Eric shook his head wearily. "There are so many people trapped in this war, on both sides. I wish it were over."

But the war was far from over. In fact, it was growing by the day as more cities fell to the Japanese. Eric got regular letters from Flo, and the news was not good. Despite the local government's best efforts, Tientsin was now firmly under Japanese occupation. Newspapers were told what they could and could not print, and most means of transportation, including the railways, and even the post office were controlled by the Japanese. To pay for their war, the Japanese were importing into China huge quantities of heroin, a highly addictive and dangerous drug; in Tientsin, and other Chinese cities, many people had become addicted.

Despite what was happening in Tientsin, Eric continually reminded himself that Flo and the girls were much safer there than out in Siao Chang with him.

In January 1939, the hospital was in crisis. It was the middle of a particularly harsh winter, and the hospital was heated by coal-fired hot-water heaters. The Japanese in the surrounding countryside decided to steal the hospital's supply of coal to keep themselves warm. On the Great Plain of North China in winter, a hospital can't function for long without heat. Something had to be done about the situation at once.

Eric volunteered to return to the London Missionary Society headquarters in Tientsin to get the money needed to buy more coal to replace what the Japanese had stolen. He knew it would be a dangerous journey that would take him through territory controlled by different armies. In one particular place, he would have to travel over a tract of land that was held by the Communists. In addition, the railway lines that ran along both sides of the land were controlled by the Japanese.

Eric set out early on a Monday morning and got into difficulty almost immediately. He was confronted by a group of Japanese soldiers who demanded to know what a foreigner was doing roaming the Chinese countryside in the dead of winter. Eric explained who he was, and the soldiers all laughed at him. They told him to take off his shoes and jacket so they could search them. They found nothing that interested them and finally let him go. But the same situation soon repeated itself, this time with Communist soldiers. It happened several more times with different patrols before Eric reached Tientsin. Eric began to wonder how he would ever make it back to Siao Chang with a large sum of money. The first men to search him would surely steal it.

After several days of train rides, cart rides, and boat rides, Eric finally made it the four hundred miles to Tientsin. Once safely there, he hurried to visit Flo and the children. It was a wonderful reunion. They had not seen each other for eight months. Four-year-old Patricia proudly showed her daddy how she could write her name, and three-year-old Heather sang every song she had learned at Sunday school. Eric loved being home again with his family.

The next day, Eric went to the London Missionary Society headquarters to report on the situation at the hospital and the need for money to buy more coal. The director told Eric that rather than take the money back to Siao Chang to buy coal, he should take a ferryboat south to Tehchow to buy coal there. Then he should hire a barge and have it towed through the rivers and canals back to Siao Chang. That way he would be able to get much more coal for the money.

Eric spent the next two days with his family. At first Heather was shy, but soon she was calling him Daddy and cuddling up on his knee. At the end of the two days, it broke Eric's heart to leave his family again, but he had no choice. The hospital had to have coal to provide heat, or many patients could die.

Eric's journey back started well. The ferryboat trip was uneventful, and Eric was able to buy a good amount of coal in Tehchow and still have some money left over. He hired a barge onto which the coal was loaded, and then he hopped aboard for the journey inland. The land alongside the river was occupied by the various armies, each of which demanded a toll from the river traffic that passed by their location. The remainder of Eric's money started to disappear as fast as it was handed over to pay tolls. Then, during the first night on the barge, something else disappeared: half the coal! Bandits had made off with it while Eric slept. Eric was discouraged but not ready to give up. The following day, though, bandits attacked again. This time Eric was held at gunpoint while the bandits took the rest of the coal from the barge. Before they left, the bandits also took the last of Eric's money. Eric had no choice. He left the barge and headed back to Tientsin to try again.

This time, Eric decided not to bring any coal back with him. It would be better to buy less coal for the money when he got back to the hospital than to arrive with a barge and no coal. Eric was also determined not to be robbed again, so he hid the money in a hollowed-out loaf of French bread that poked innocently from the top of his knapsack. The trip turned out to be uneventful until about seventy miles from Siao Chang. The train Eric was riding on suddenly shuddered to a halt. Eric and the other passengers climbed out to see what the problem was, hoping it was nothing serious, as it was snowing outside and they did not want to be stopped for long. Eric couldn't see very far in front of him because of the snow, but news filtered back to where he stood stomping his feet to keep warm. It was bad news. Some Chinese peasants had sabotaged the railroad tracks as a way to get back at the Japanese. They had torn up a large section of the rails, and a freight train had run off the end of the tracks and lay in a crumpled heap directly in front of them.

Soon the conductor confirmed that this was indeed what had happened. He then told the passengers that the train would back up to the last station they had passed and wait for the tracks to be repaired, though no one seemed to know how long that would be. If any of the passengers wanted to continue with their journey, they would have to walk along the torn-up tracks and wait at the other end for another train, which would then back up in the direction they were headed. Eric knew he had to keep going; the need for coal at the hospital was serious by now, so he swung his knapsack with the French bread still sticking out of it onto his back and headed up the tracks with a dozen other passengers.

Eric pulled the collar of his woolen coat around his face and braced himself against the cutting wind. The snow whipped into his eyes, making it hard to see. Eric and the other passengers formed a line and followed the bumps of the railroad ties that were visible in the snow. They walked on and on, mile after mile.

Finally, six miles from where they had started walking, they reached the end of the torn-up section of tracks. They soon realized, however, that they would have to walk on until they came to a station. If they waited for a train to come to the end of the tracks it might be derailed and wrecked just like the freight train had been. They kept walking until they would reach a station where the train would stop and they could tell the engineer to back up. It was another three miles to the station. It was getting colder, and night was falling when they arrived at the station. It was not the type of station Eric had hoped for. There was no building to shelter in—just a sign and a platform.

Eric and his fellow travelers slumped onto the platform. They huddled together to keep warm and constantly glanced down the railroad tracks, hoping to see a train. They had to wait through the night until around noon the following day before they finally heard the unmistakable rumble of a steam engine through the silence of the snow-draped countryside.

The train stopped beside the station platform. The engineer was surprised to see a group of snow-covered people huddling together for warmth. He was not surprised, though, to hear about the torn-up railroad tracks. An army needs supplies, and destroying the tracks to prevent trains from getting through to the front lines was an easy way to hurt the Japanese.

Eric climbed onto the train and collapsed into a seat. He just wanted to get back to the hospital so that he could sleep. The train began to back up, and three hours later, Eric recognized the station at Siao Chang. He had made it back safely, and with all the money. From the station he hired a cart to take him to the hospital compound.

At the hospital, Eric reached into his knapsack and pulled out the loaf of French bread. He ripped it open, and a bundle of money fell out. After counting it, he proudly handed it over to the hospital director. It had been a difficult mission, but he had succeeded.

In fact, he had done such a good job he was asked to do it again. Two days later, Eric was sitting on a mule cart headed back to Tientsin. This time his assignment was to collect desperately needed medical supplies for the hospital.

Although still exhausted from the stress of the previous trip, Eric was excited. He could hardly wait to get to Tientsin. Before he set out, the hospital director had released him to take a long-awaited furlough with Flo and the girls as soon as the supplies had been safely delivered to the hospital. Eric was eager to tell Flo the good news. How wonderful it would be to spend a year away from the constant stress of war.

Eric made plans in his head for the furlough as he rumbled along on the mule cart. But he had no way of knowing then that far from leaving war behind when he and Flo and the two girls took their furlough, they would be headed into another war, a different war, a war that would nearly cost all four of them their lives.

Chapter 13

Across the Ocean

"Is the whole world at war?" Florence Liddell asked her husband as they sat on the doorstep of her parents' home in Toronto, Canada.

"It certainly seems like it," replied Eric, reaching to put his arm around his wife. They both looked down at their two little daughters playing happily in their grandmother's garden.

Eric sighed deeply. He had arrived in Canada just in time to hear the worst possible news. On September 3, 1939, Britain and France had declared war on Germany, starting what would become the Second World War. Seven days later, Canada also declared war on Germany. It felt to Eric, as he sat on the doorstep in the hot afternoon sun, that his whole life had been punctuated by war. The Boxer

Rebellion was in progress when he was born, World War I occurred while he was attending high school, and the Sino-Japanese War had been in progress most of his married life. And now there was a new war in Europe.

At least there was no threat of fighting in Canada, so Eric decided to leave Flo and the girls in Toronto for several months while he went on to the United Kingdom. There he would give a full report of his work in China at the London Missionary Society headquarters in London and then do the expected public speaking in churches and at clubs. When this was all done, Flo, Patricia, and Heather would join Eric in Scotland, where they would have five months to rest and spend time with Eric's mother, Jenny, and Ernest.

All went as planned. Before heading for London, Eric visited his mother in Edinburgh. They both thought the other had changed. Eric was shocked to see that his mother, whom he had not seen for nine years, had aged considerably. His mother now had white hair and seemed to be shorter than ever. She was glad to see Eric and hear all about his family. Even though Eric had written to her every week and told her most things in his letters, there was something about sharing family news in person. She told Eric he looked balder than ever and joked that his baldness probably wasn't due to too many hot showers after all. She also said that he was quieter than he had been on his last furlough. After she had heard some of the things he had experienced in Siao

Chang, she understood why. Living in a war zone was very sobering. She herself had lived through the ravages of the Boxer Rebellion in China.

The time passed quickly for Eric. He was just as popular as ever, but the crowds that gathered to hear him speak as he toured Scotland, England, and Wales behaved differently from those of nine years before. They listened carefully as he spoke about his war experiences, and they asked him what it was like to live under occupation and how the enemy had treated him. Eric answered their questions as best he could, sensing they were searching for answers about what their own futures might hold. No one could be sure what Adolf Hitler, fuhrer from Nazi Germany, would do next. Already Hitler's troops had overrun and occupied large portions of Europe, and people in Great Britain were wondering whether it might be the next country to be captured.

In March 1940, Florence and the girls joined Eric. They spent five wonderful months in Scotland. Grannie Liddell finally got to meet her two granddaughters. She loved to read to them and fuss over them. Meanwhile, Aunt Jenny took her two nieces shopping for fabric and made them each new dresses for the trip back to China.

While home, the family also attended Elsa McKechnie's wedding. It was a wonderful day filled with memories for Eric. The schoolgirl who had started the Official Eric Liddell Fan Club was now a married woman.

Finally, the time came for the four of them to return to China. It was the hardest parting ever for Eric. His mother was getting old, and he had a strange feeling he would never see her again. The girls had also loved the attention of their extended family, and no one was sure what kind of country they might return to on their next furlough.

To return to China, the Liddells planned to sail across the Atlantic Ocean to Nova Scotia, Canada, then take a train to Toronto to say good-bye to Flo's parents. From there they would continue on by train across Canada to the Pacific Coast, where they would board another ship for the trip across the Pacific Ocean to China. There was just one problem. Now that Great Britain was at war with Germany, no vessel crossing the Atlantic Ocean was safe. German submarines, or U-boats, as they were called, had orders to sink any ship flying the British flag. It made no difference whether it was a navy ship or a privately owned merchant vessel. German U-boats had already sunk many British ships.

Since crossing the Atlantic Ocean by ship had become such a risky business, two important safety measures had been put in place. First, all ships now traveled in convoys, that is, large groups of vessels all sailing together. In so doing, ships were able to help each other keep a lookout for U-boats and rescue survivors from any ship unlucky enough to be torpedoed. Second, all convoys were escorted by battleships from the Royal Navy until they were two days out from the coast of Great Britain. The U-boats did not have the equipment on board for long voyages, and so most of the time they stayed within two days' sailing of the coast.

The Liddells traveled to Liverpool, where they boarded the small ship that would take them across the Atlantic Ocean. Three hundred other passengers and crew were aboard. Eric studied the ship carefully as he climbed the gangway to board her. The ship looked seaworthy enough, and perhaps being so small, she would be hard to hit with a torpedo from a U-boat.

Fifty ships were in the convoy, and it took a little coordinating to get them all collected into a flotilla. The ships formed five lines of ten ships each. The Liddells' ship was near the back of the middle line of ships. In formation, the ships all sailed through the Irish Sea, around the south coast of Ireland, and out into the Atlantic. Their escort of Royal Navy warships steamed along beside the two outside rows of ships.

As they sat outside after dinner on their first night, Eric marveled at how strange it was to be sailing in a convoy. Every time he'd made a trip on a ship before, the vessel had been sailing alone on a large ocean. On several occasions, Eric had completed an entire voyage without seeing another ship. But now, here he was on a ship surrounded by many other ships. It felt like they were part of a floating city.

Eric and Flo had just finished tucking the girls into their bunks that night when they felt an enormous jolt, and the whole ship shuddered. Eric told Flo to stay with the girls while he sprinted up on deck to see what had happened, although he already had a good idea. The deck was swarming with passengers, all asking the same question. Eventually, they gathered in the dining room, where the first officer joined them. The officer announced that the captain was sure that the ship had been struck by a torpedo, but for some reason the weapon had not exploded. The captain did not think it had done any structural damage to the ship, but they had gone to red alert just in case. All of the ships in the convoy were going to start zigzag maneuvers. Eric knew that ships under attack zigzagged to make them harder targets. He raced below deck to tell Flo the news.

Nothing further happened that night, but two mornings later, they awoke to bad news. One of the ships at the back of the convoy had been sunk during the night. Later that morning, everyone aboard watched quietly as the Royal Navy warships that had escorted them out into the Atlantic Ocean left the convoy and headed back towards England. They were now forty-nine ships alone in a hostile ocean. They were hopeful, though, that they were now out of range of German U-boats.

Nervously, the convoy moved forward. The sea had become rough, which everyone aboard knew make it difficult to spot submarines. At 11 A.M., the passengers and crew heard a loud boom. Looking in the direction of the sound, they saw a cloud of black smoke rising above the waves. The ship's horn began to sound, and everyone on deck knew what the signal meant. The passengers hurried to grab their lifejackets. Eric and Flo struggled to get Patricia and Heather into theirs. Even though the ship had children's sized lifejackets, the jackets were still much too big for Patricia and Heather, causing their arms to stick straight out from their sides.

Half an hour later, the passengers were all sitting in neat rows on deck in front of the lifeboats, ready to abandon ship at a moment's notice. The entire convoy was zigzagging trying to outwit the U-boat that was patrolling farther out in the Atlantic Ocean than expected. News soon spread among the passengers and crew that the ship at the back of their line had been sunk. The torpedo had probably hit the ship in the boiler, because the ship had exploded and gone down in less than two minutes, too quickly for anyone to be saved.

The passengers sat on deck for three hours before the captain gave the all clear signal. They were then allowed to enter the dining room for lunch. No sooner had Eric lifted Heather into her highchair than the ship's horn blared out again. Someone yelled that the radio officer had received a message that another ship had been hit by a torpedo, and everyone rushed out to the lifeboats again. Eric and Flo tried to keep their children calm. Since everything about the ship and its routine was new to the girls, they did not find it strange at all to be sitting on the deck in rows. Eric smiled as he played with Patricia; for all she knew, this could be what people always did aboard ship!

By this time, it seemed to Eric that the ships were in more danger bunched up in a convoy than they would be as lone ships on a big ocean. Apparently the captains of the ships agreed, because at about 3 P.M., the word was given for the ships to fall out of formation and each one to make her own way to Canada.

The Liddell family sat with the other passengers and watched the ships steam away that had flanked them port and starboard for two-and-a-half days. Soon not a single ship was in sight. Everyone was still sitting on deck at 6 P.M. when another message came over the ship's radio. The ship that had been sailing parallel to theirs on the port side in the convoy had been torpedoed and was sinking. Flo squeezed Eric's hand when the passengers heard the news. She and Eric both knew it could just as easily have been their ship that was hit and was sinking.

Ten minutes later, they received almost the same message, only this time it was a different ship that had been torpedoed and sunk. Eric began to wonder whether he and his family would all die at sea. Their ship steamed on hour after hour, straining for every bit of speed. The captain hoped that he had outrun the last U-boat, but he couldn't be sure. That night, the passengers were told to sleep on the deck fully dressed and wearing their lifejackets. They were each given a few minutes to run below to get blankets and pillows from their cabin. It was a long night. The seas were still rough, and the ship lurched from side to side as she continued to maintain a zigzag pattern.

The next morning, the sea was calmer, and everyone felt a little safer. The ship was well out of U-boat range. Only a large seagoing submarine could torpedo her now, but such ships did not prowl that far north in the Atlantic Ocean.

Three days later was Canadian Thanksgiving Day. That morning, the captain asked Eric to conduct a special service. Everyone aboard had a lot to be thankful for. The ship was still afloat and now not far from her destination.

Also that morning, Patricia and Heather awoke with red dots on their faces. They had measles. This meant more complications for the Liddells, since people arriving in Canada from a foreign country had to go into quarantine if they were sick. When the ship finally docked in Nova Scotia, the family was ordered into a Red Cross center instead of traveling on to Flo's parents' home. Since there was no bedding at the center, once again everyone slept in his or her clothes. The following morning the family was released and allowed to travel on to Toronto.

The Liddells had a short visit with Flo's parents in Toronto. They would like to have stayed longer, but they were due back in China by the end of October. Mr. and Mrs. McKenzie did not try to dissuade their daughter and son-in-law from returning to China, but they did worry about their safety. From what they had heard from their missionary friends still living there, China was becoming a more dangerous place with each passing day.

Chapter 14

Enemies

The Siao Chang to which Eric returned at the end of October 1940 was not the same place he had left a year before. A high wall now surrounded the entire town, which was patrolled day and night by guards. The Japanese had decided to occupy Siao Chang and turn it into a garrison town and command center for road building in the area.

Until that time, the roads that linked the villages on the Great Plain were narrow, winding, and unpaved. They wound carefully around gardens and ancient cemeteries. Cemeteries were very important to the Chinese people of the Great Plain. The people carefully tended and protected them, that is, until the Japanese decided that straight, paved roads across the plain would help them get their troops and provisions from one place to another faster. Such new roads would be wide enough and flat enough for motor vehicles instead of the customary carts and mules. Motor vehicles and tanks, the Japanese hoped, would help them win the war. All able-bodied men, women, and children in Siao Chang were forced to help build the new roads. They shoveled dirt and moved huge rocks by hand. The work was both backbreaking, and heartbreaking. While the Japanese guards played cards and told each other jokes, their Chinese forced laborers were made to hack roads through the most sacred thing in their lives: their ancestors' graves.

Eric felt sick when he heard what the Japanese had done. He was glad he had come back. The Chinese people now more than ever needed some good news. Somehow they had to find meaning in their lives in the midst of such cruelty and hatred. Eric knew that the truth of the gospel message could give them that meaning.

Some things did go on as "normal," though. Couples were married, babies were born, and funeral services were held. Soon after he had returned, Eric was invited to a nearby village to attend the wedding of a couple he knew well. The ceremony went fine, and the wedding party paid no attention to the blast of heavy artillery less than a mile away. In the joy of the wedding, the outside world was ignored for a few hours.

Eric had planned to return to Siao Chang later that night after the wedding. However, when he heard that the Communist army was out in force, he decided to spend the night. The next morning he set out for home on his bicycle. A friend who had also attended the wedding rode with him. They were about halfway to Siao Chang when Eric heard the ping of bullets around him. Immediately, he slammed on his brakes and yelled for his friend to do the same. Both men jumped off their bicycles, and as they did so, more bullets whizzed around them. Then suddenly the hail of bullets abruptly stopped. Eric and his friend heard a rustle in the bushes at the side off the road, and several Chinese men sheepishly crawled out of the undergrowth. They immediately began apologizing to Eric and his friend. Apparently, they had mistaken the two of them on their bicycles for members of the Japanese army. As Eric and his friend leapt from their bikes, the Chinese men were able to get a good look at them, realized their mistake, and stopped firing. After they had apologized, Eric and his friend rode on. As he rode, Eric thought about what had happened. No one was safe anymore. Something as simple as riding back from a wedding could get a person killed. Eric was just glad the Chinese men had been such poor shots!

Eric wrote often to Flo in Tientsin. In his letters he tried to explain to her how things had changed in Siao Chang and how important he felt his missionary work was. "I now go to the southwest to a part I never visited before. When I am out it is giving, giving, giving all the time, and trying to get to know the people, and trying to leave them a message of encouragement and peace in a time when there is no external peace at all," he wrote in one letter to Flo.

The closer the Japanese forces got to completing their roads, the worse their behavior got. Officers no longer seemed to care about keeping their troops in order. Drunken soldiers would lurch into the hospital looking for patients or nurses to harass, their long swords gleaming menacingly at their sides. Many villages around Siao Chang were bombed to the ground, and a constant stream of injured and dying people entered the hospital. So many people needed medical help that Eric was pressed into service in the hospital as a nursing assistant. He learned to boil surgical instruments to sterilize them and to change dressings like an expert. He enjoyed his work in the hospital; it gave him time to share his faith with the patients. But there were dangers, too.

One day Annie Buchan, hospital matron, walked into the operating theater looking for a doctor. She found him pinned against a wall with a Japanese soldier beating him over the head with a baton. Annie sprang forward without thinking. "I want this doctor," she demanded loudly.

Startled to be spoken to in such a way by a short, white woman, the soldier stepped back and then stormed out of the room. Annie tended to the doctor's wounds. Although the situation ended "happily," the hospital staff, including Eric, began to wonder about their long-term safety as the situation around them continued to worsen.

Finally, five months after Eric returned to Siao Chang, the Japanese ordered all foreigners out of the area. The hospital that had treated anyone in need, including Japanese soldiers, had to be evacuated. The missionaries were given two weeks to get out and told they could take nothing with them. As the missionaries left, they handed the keys of the hospital over to the Japanese, wondering what would happen to the sick and wounded people of the district now that there was no one to take care of them. It was obvious that the Japanese would not open the building up as a hospital again. In fact, it was never used again. Several months later, the building was burned to the ground.

The London Missionary Society staff from Siao Chang scattered. Some, like Eric's brother Robert and his family, took long overdue furloughs while others went to work in different hospitals and clinics. Some, like Eric, went to Tientsin. Back in Tientsin, Eric had a long talk with Flo. It was obvious that the Japanese were becoming more hostile towards Europeans, and Eric did not feel that it was safe for Flo to stay in China any longer, especially now that she was expecting their third child. There were also rumors that the Japanese were considering ordering all foreigners into internment camps. Eric could not bear the thought of his wife giving birth under such conditions. At first Flo was reluctant to leave, but in the end, she came to agree with

Eric. It would be much safer for her and the girls back in Canada. When the war was finally over, she would return to China.

Escorting Flo and his daughters to the ship that would take them to Canada was probably the most difficult thing Eric Liddell ever had to do in his life. Five-year-old Patricia skipped along beside him as they climbed the gangway to board the ship, and Heather gave him a big grin when he lifted her onto the top bunk in their cabin. Before Eric and Flo had time to say everything they wanted to say to each other, the ship's whistle sounded. It was the signal for all visitors to disembark so that the gangway could be lowered and the ship made ready to sail.

Eric sat on the bottom bunk and pulled Patricia onto his knee. He looked into her big blue eyes, which were almost identical to his own. "Now, Tricia," he said, choking back tears. "I want you to look after Mummy and help her with Heather and the new baby."

Patricia gave him a big hug. "Yes, Daddy, I'll take care of Mummy until you come back," she said bravely.

Flo turned away so that the children would not see her tears.

Hand in hand, the family finally walked back out onto deck, where Eric kissed his wife good-bye. He gave her one last hug and whispered in her ear, "Those who love God never meet for the last time."

Flo nodded as she fought back her tears. She knew she had to be strong, both for Eric and for the children.

After the ship had sailed, Eric returned to Tientsin with a heavy heart. He was sure he had done the right thing sending his family away to safety, but it had been so difficult to say good-bye, not knowing exactly when he would see them again. Since he could not go back to Siao Chang, Eric stayed with a teacher from the Anglo-Chinese college. Once again he was living in the French concession, where he had spent so many happy times with his parents and family when he had first returned to China.

Eric did not return to teaching. The school year at the Anglo-Chinese college was already under way, and the school did not need any extra teachers. For the first time in a long while, Eric had nothing in particular to do, so he decided to pursue a dream he'd had for a long time. There was little written material available to instruct Chinese pastors in how to effectively lead their churches, and Eric wanted to write a simple manual that would provide such instruction. He began his *Manual of Christian Discipleship* and worked hard on it every day. He also spoke at many church services and meetings.

Eric was still working on the manual in September when he received a telegram from Flo, who had given birth to a baby girl. Eric longed to see Flo and hold Maureen Liddell, his newest daughter, but he knew it was not yet the right time. Things were getting worse in China, and as a missionary, he had a vital message of hope and encouragement that needed to be shared with people during such a dark time.

December 1941 was not a good month for foreigners in China. On December 7, three hundred fifty Japanese aircraft bombed Pearl Harbor on the Hawaiian island of Oahu, where the American Pacific Fleet was anchored. Two battleships were sunk, and six others were severely damaged. Nearly 2,900 American soldiers and sailors were killed. The same day, the Japanese also attacked the Philippines and British-controlled Malaya and Hong Kong. The following day, December 8, 1941, the United States and Great Britain declared war on Japan.

The world was shocked at the way Japan had launched such vicious attacks. All but the Chinese, who were already well acquainted with the full wrath of Japan's vicious determination to control them. But the rest of the world had largely ignored the fighting in China. Indeed, the Sino-Japanese War was often referred to as the "Forgotten War" because so few outsiders took any interest in it.

After the Pearl Harbor attack, Japanese troops in China became much more hostile towards foreigners, especially the British and Americans, who were now officially "the enemy." Because of the changed attitude towards foreigners, the London Missionary Society wanted all its missionaries together in one place. It asked Eric and six other men to leave the French concession and relocate into the English concession. Eric was invited to live with the Howard-Smith family. He made the move to their home none too soon. Within days, electrified barricades were erected around the concessions, and

Japanese soldiers manned all the gates in and out of them. The Japanese ordered all foreigners to remain inside the concession they were living in. There was to be no more moving about from concession to concession or into the city of Tientsin itself. Nor were there to be any more large meetings held. Any gathering of over ten people was banned.

This ban on meetings posed a challenge for Eric, who had been holding regular church services in the British concession. People from all walks of life, diplomats and textile mill owners, sea captains, teachers, and missionaries, were living there. As the situation in China deteriorated, these people were beginning to worry about what the future might hold for them. They needed comfort and reassurance, and Eric held his regular church service as a way to provide them. And now, when these people needed even more comfort and reassurance in the face of increased Japanese hostility, Eric was being told that he could no longer hold his church services, at least not with more than ten people present.

Eric thought about the problem for a long time and finally came up with a solution. He decided to continue preparing a sermon each week, but instead of preaching the sermon from the pulpit, he wrote it out. Then he enlisted the help of another missionary's wife, who invited nine people over for afternoon tea. While her guests sipped their tea, the missionary's wife handed out copies of Eric's sermon, and together they read and discussed it. Then each of those nine people invited another nine people to their home for afternoon tea and handed out copies of the sermon, which they read and discussed. Then each of those nine did the same for another nine people, and so it went on. In this way, it did not take long before everyone in the concession had heard the week's sermon, and all without breaking the Japanese order not to hold large public meetings. Eric's solution became known as the "Afternoon-Tea Church."

Meanwhile, the Reverend and Mrs. Howard-Smith loved having Eric stay with them. In 100-degree heat, Eric taught their daughters how to play tennis. He also played cricket with them and made up the fourth player if they wanted to play bridge. He showed the girls his stamp collection, and when they got excited about starting one of their own, he spent hours ruling up stamp albums for them. Nothing seemed too much trouble for him. When food supplies in the concession ran low and Mrs. Howard-Smith had difficulty buying bread, Eric volunteered to get in line at the bakery at five o'clock every morning to make sure the family got some.

In a letter to a friend, the Reverend Howard-Smith wrote, "I never saw Eric angry. I never heard him say a cross or unkind word. He just went about doing good."

By August 1942, Eric was beginning to think that his time in China was nearly over. He had finished the manual he'd been writing, and since he could not leave the British concession, he couldn't see much point in staying in China. The Japanese had promised that before 1942 had ended, they would grant permission to leave the concessions to anyone who wanted to return to his or her home country. Eric wrote to Flo and explained the situation. He wondered what she thought about the idea of his continuing his pastoral work in Canada. There was plenty of hard work to be done there spreading the gospel message. Flo wrote back to tell him she thought it was a wonderful idea for him to come to Canada. She also told him that Patricia and Heather had both started school and that ten-month-old Maureen was growing and thriving. The letter lifted Eric's spirits. He could hardly wait to get to Canada and see his family again and begin a new life with them there.

August dragged into September, and September into October. There were many rumors, but no firm word, as to when the Japanese would allow foreigners to leave the concessions to return home. New Year's Day 1943 came and went, and still no news. There was no news until lunchtime March 12, 1943. But it was not the news Eric or anyone else had been expecting. All British and American "enemies" were to report to Weihsien Internment Camp in the center of Shantung Province, four hundred miles southeast of Tientsin. No "enemies" would be allowed to leave China to return to their home country.

The foreign enemies were given two weeks to prepare for their internment. Each person was allowed to send three trunks and a bed and bedding ahead to the camp. As he loaded his bed onto a waiting Japanese truck, Eric wondered whether he would ever see it again or whether it was just a Japanese ploy to steal beds for their troops. Those to be interned were also to be allowed to carry two pieces of luggage with them to the camp. The Japanese divided the people in the British concession into three groups and made Eric captain of one of the groups. The groups would be transported to the internment camp one at a time over three consecutive days. Eric's group was scheduled to leave on March 30.

As the day approached, Eric looked at his belongings and wondered what were the best things to take to an internment camp. What would it be like there? Should he prepare for a short stay or a long one? Which was more important, an extra set of clothes or a supply of canned meat, a kettle or a set of encyclopedias? Would he be housed in a dormitory or a cell? The more Eric considered it all, the more questions he had about what lay ahead for him and the other enemies of the Japanese.

Chapter 15

The Courtyard of the Happy Way

At 7:30 P.M. on March 30, 1943, the last group of people left in the British concession gathered near the guard house. There were about three hundred of them, and they looked like a group of rich tourists going on an outing. Many of the women wore heavy mink coats and fashionable high heels. Under their coats they wore beautifully tailored woolen suits. Pearl necklaces and diamond earrings completed their outfits. The men wore suits with starched-collared shirts and striped ties. They all seemed to have far too much luggage with them. There were piles of beach chairs, hat boxes, canteens of silver cutlery, even a set of golf clubs!

Eric couldn't help but smile to himself as he viewed the sight. They all seemed to have such different ideas of what they would find at the end of their journey, and these ideas were reflected in how the people dressed and what they brought with them.

A few small children wove in and out of the group as they waited. Some of the timid children clutched well-worn teddy bears or held their mothers' hands tightly. The more adventurous ones clambered over the piles of belongings. They all waited for an hour before the Japanese commander finally arrived and began barking orders. "Everyone, pick up belongings and proceed to railway station. Follow that guard," he yelled.

A gasp went up from the group. Did the Japanese really expect them to carry all of their luggage themselves? It was three miles to the railway station.

"How dare they?" whispered one well-dressed woman to her husband. "Tell him we want to hire a Chinese servant to carry our luggage for us."

Eric watched as her husband shook his head. "We'll just have to leave what we cannot manage, Ethel," he replied glumly.

"Now!" bellowed the Japanese commander above the noise of the crowd. "Go now. Hurry, hurry."

Eric picked up his two bags and began the trek to the train station. He felt grateful in a way. He had lived out on the Great Plain and had experienced the hardship of war firsthand. He had gone hungry, been shot at, and slept on dirt floors. Most of the people around him had never experienced anything like it. Most of them had led pampered colonial lives. They'd had servants to do their washing, servants to run their baths, servants to make their beds and cook their meals. They'd had chauffeurs to run their wives to bridge parties and chauffeurs to pick up their children from exclusive private schools. For every task they had found unpleasant, boring, or time-consuming, there had been a Chinese servant pleased to earn a few pennies doing it. But that lifestyle had come to an abrupt end, and Eric wondered how these people were going to adjust to the new life that lay ahead of them.

The group trudged through the gates of the British concession for the last time. Eric glanced behind him. A pile of belongings sat by the side of the road; virtually everything that Eric or anyone else in the group owned, if it had not been sent ahead to the camp, had been abandoned. Hand-carved mahogany dining tables, glistening chandeliers, collections of hunting rifles, and libraries filled with first-edition leather-bound books had all been left behind. Within days, it would all be looted from their houses and sold on the black market.

Eric walked in silence. Many of the women around him wept quietly as they marched in two lines down the street. Chinese people stood on both sides of the road. Many of them bowed slightly as the foreigners straggled by. The Chinese people were in a difficult position. Most of them resented the concessions and the way foreigners made so much money off their country. But at the same time, the British were their allies against the Japanese. In this war at least, the two were on the same side.

It took an hour for the group to reach the station. Once there, they were told to wait for the train that would take them on the four hundred-mile journey to Weihsien Internment Camp.

No one said much as the train puffed into view pulling a row of third-class carriages. When the train came to a halt, the British prisoners were herded inside. Too many people were crammed into the filthy carriages for anyone to get comfortable. Some people sat on suitcases while others perched on straight-backed wooden benches. Babies cried, and toddlers whined for their beds and their dinners.

Eric sat on his bags in the aisle and watched his fellow travelers. They were all British, they spoke English, and they were all on their way to an internment camp, but that was all they had in common with each other. All of them were from varied walks of life and social classes. Many of them had never ever before had to mix with each other. Now they sat silently side by side staring grimly out at the darkness that had settled over the countryside. Eric prayed silently as the train rolled along through the night. "God, help me to shine Your light among these people."

The train took sixteen exhausting hours to reach Weihsien. Stiff and sleepless, the passengers climbed awkwardly from the train. They were then told the internment camp was two miles outside the city. Whispers went around the group. According to those who had visited Weihsien before, they were probably going to be interned at the American Presbyterian Mission Station just outside of town.

Since there were no trucks to take them the two miles to the camp, once again they all picked up their luggage and began to walk. Eric shifted his luggage from one hand to the other as he walked along. Then, finally, the gate to the American Presbyterian Mission Station came into view. The rumor was true. This was where they were going to be interned. As Eric walked up to the gate, he noticed the sign in Chinese hanging above it. He translated it out loud as he walked under it: "The Courtyard of the Happy Way." No one was happy to be in the courtyard that night!

Inside the gates, Japanese guards led the group along a pathway between two buildings and out into a small open field with a rugby goalpost at one end. When the group had gathered on the field, one of the guards pointed to a tall, dark-haired European man with glasses. The men stepped in front of the group and turned to address it. "Welcome to Weihsien Internment Camp," he began in a clipped English accent. "I know you will have many questions, but the one thing we have here is plenty of time to answer them." He gave a little chuckle at his own joke, but no one else seemed to find it funny. He continued. "For now, I am going to tell you that including yourselves, there are about eighteen hundred of us here. We come from three cities, Peking, Tsingtao, and, of course, Tientsin. We are placed in dormitories according to where we come from, and there are three kitchens within the compound, so each group gets to cook for itself and eat together. Now, if you would separate into families on the right and singles on the left, we can get you settled into a room, and then you can get your dinner."

Eric shuffled to the left. In some ways, he envied the people on the right; they were families and could comfort and support each other. But in other ways, he hated the thought of his wife and daughters being in an internment camp.

"One more thing," said the man, raising his clipped English voice above the crowd. "The bathrooms are to your right in the long, low building. They're not in great shape yet...." His voice trailed off apologetically.

Eric and five other men were directed to one of the dormitory buildings. One of the men was A. P. Cullen, who had been a teacher at Eltham College in London when Eric was a young student there. A. P. Cullen had also been a fellow teacher with Eric at the Anglo-Chinese college. On the way to the dormitory, the men stopped by the bathrooms. Eric almost wished they hadn't. He had been in China long enough to experience many types of bathrooms, but the one he saw, or smelled, when he opened the door was a hundred times worse than anything he'd seen before. It was easy to see the bathrooms had once been the sparkling-clean pride of the janitor of the Presbyterian Mission Station. The toilet bowls were all new and sunk low into the ground like all Chinese toilets. Above each bowl dangled a polished bronze chain, which when pulled should have produced a flush of water. But therein was the problem. All the water pipes in the toilet had been ripped out, and the toilet bowls were already backed up and overflowing. A man in the bathroom explained that there was no running water in the whole camp, no plumber to repair the pipes, and no Chinese servants to clean up the mess.

At that moment, Eric grasped the enormity of what lay ahead. Somehow the eighteen hundred people interned in the camp, cut off from families, friends, and countries, would have to find a way to work together to form a community. It was going to have to be a community where many people would need to do jobs they had never even dreamed of doing before. They were going to have to cook meals, clean toilets, pump water, and hand wash clothes. Eric sighed. It was going to be quite an unusual experience for many of the people in the camp who were used to being pampered by Chinese servants.

Eric did not spend long in his new dorm room. There was absolutely no furniture in the room and no sign of the bed he had loaded onto a Japanese truck several days before in Tientsin. He shoved his bags up against a wall and headed outside again. It had turned into a cloudy, damp night, and he could hear people coughing as he walked past the doors to other dorm rooms.

The beam of a searchlight mounted on the compound wall constantly crisscrossed the camp. As it moved across the area outside the dormitory, it illuminated a pile of shattered furniture and bent pipes. The Japanese had apparently completely demolished the compound before making it an internment camp.

Eric stepped past the pile of broken furniture and walked to the wall at the north end of the compound. He decided to measure the compound. His years of running had made him fairly accurate at measuring distances with strides. He stared at the corner of the north wall and walked in a westerly direction. "One, two, three…" he counted aloud until he reached the opposite corner. One hundred fifty yards. Then he strode along the west wall in a southerly direction. Two hundred yards. Eric let out a low whistle. The entire compound was only one hundred fifty yards wide and two hundred yards long. That was only the size of two rugby fields. And into that space were packed eighteen hundred people.

The realization shocked Eric. How could people get any privacy when they were crowded in so tightly? And how long were they going to have to remain crammed together in the camp?

Eric was still thinking about this when A. P. Cullen grabbed his arm. "You'd better get in line for dinner, or you'll miss out," he said, pulling Eric towards a pool of light. Soon Eric was in line with five hundred other people. They were all from Tientsin, and they were all hungry. Only those who had carried food with them from the

British concession had eaten anything in the past twenty-four hours, and Eric was not one of them.

Slowly the line edged towards a woman with a huge pot of liquid that she was ladling into bowls.

"Where do you get the bowls?" Eric asked a man in front of him.

"You bring them with you, of course," he replied, producing his own bowl from a bag he had slung over his shoulder.

Eric and A. P. Cullen looked at each other and groaned. Why hadn't they noticed sooner? They had been standing in line for a half hour by then. They both slipped out of line and walked quickly back to their room. Fortunately, both of them had plates and silverware packed away in their bags. Others, though, were not so lucky. They had not packed any plates and had to find people who would lend them some so they could eat. Their plight got Eric wondering. He might have brought plates, but what other important things had he forgotten to bring?

When he got back to the line, it was moving more quickly, and within ten minutes he and A. P. Cullen were sitting with their backs against a brick wall eating soup and chunks of bread. Eric looked around. This was the kind of meal most of the British people from the concession would have refused to eat had it been served to them at home or in a restaurant. Now they had no choice. Now they were prisoners in an internment camp, surrounded by high walls and barbed wire.

After dinner, Eric and A. P. Cullen, along with just about everyone else in the camp, headed for bed. Those who had arrived by train that day were exhausted. Most had hardly slept the night before. Eric slept in his clothes on the hard floor. There seemed little point changing into pajamas when there was no bed to curl up in.

The next morning, Eric got up an hour earlier than everyone else, and as he did each morning, he used the time to read his Bible and pray. At exactly 7:15 A.M. a horn blared out, signaling that it was fifteen minutes to roll call. Eric pulled on an extra sweater and headed outside. It was a crisp morning, and he was eager to learn more about the camp in the light of day.

Eric learned a lot that first day. He learned that at least fifteen nationalities were represented in the camp. The one thing they had in common was that the Japanese army did not want them moving freely around China anymore. As expected, there were large numbers of people from Great Britain and the United States, but there were also people from Italy, Belgium, Holland, India, Palestine, Russia, and Cuba. Some had lived most of their lives in China; some were the children or grandchildren of merchants and businessmen who had immigrated to China many years before. Others, like the jazz duo consisting of a native Hawaiian and a black American, or the two Cuban families who had been touring China with a baseball team, had intended to visit the country for only a couple of weeks. They were stunned to find themselves prisoners in an internment camp. The Cuban families spoke only Spanish and had no one else to talk to.

As Eric acquired this information, he realized that language was going to be a major problem in the camp. It would be very difficult to organize things when people did not understand what was being said. Eric also learned that inside the compound the Japanese had decided to let them all pretty much alone. They had made it clear, though, that they wanted those in the camp to do their own chores and run their own affairs. By the end of his first day, Eric knew that this was going to be an extremely difficult task. How would people be motivated to work, and how would their spirits be kept up? In particular, Eric worried about the hundreds of children and teenagers he had seen that day. What was there for them to do week after week? And what about the schooling they were missing?

But as he wondered, Eric's mind kept coming back to the unanswered question that really mattered, the question that was on everyone's mind: How long were they all going to be crammed together in Weihsien Internment Camp?

No one that day could have imagined that they would be interned for two years and one month and that during that time they would become a community of people who learned to work together for the common good of everyone in the camp. And they certainly could not have predicted the fate of the forty-three-year-old athlete who would become one of the strongest and most willing workers within their prison community.

Chapter 16

Uncle Eric

Three weeks went by before the convoy of trucks arrived carrying the beds and other belongings of the British internees from Tientsin arrived. Eric had given up all hope of ever seeing his bed or trunks again, so he was very surprised when the trucks drove through the front gate. He assembled his bed and placed the mattress on top. Then he slid the three trunks that contained mostly household items under the bed.

When he was done, Eric sat on the bed and watched enviously as one of the other men in his dorm room put together a double bed. What luxury! And what foresight, though the man hadn't really planned it that way. Back in Tientsin, he'd had no single bed, so when the Japanese came to collect the beds to transport to Weihsien, he gave them the only bed he could lay his hands on. It just happened to be a double bed. Now, in the cramped confines of Weihsien Internment Camp, a double bed meant that he could claim double the amount of space in the room as his own, and he had double the area to stretch out in and sleep at night. Eric wished he'd thought to send a double bed instead of the single one he was sitting on. Still, he couldn't complain; his single bed was going to be a lot more comfortable to sleep on than the hard floorboards he'd been sleeping on for the past three weeks.

By this time, the internees had set up nine major departments in the camp: Accommodation, Discipline, Education, Employment, Engineering, Entertainment, Finances, General Affairs, and Medicine. Since a number of nurses and doctors were among the missionaries interned, for the first few days, everyone worked hard to get the hospital up and running again. Some of the equipment was still intact, but a lot of it had been so badly damaged it was no longer of any use. Several people had arrived at the camp sick, and they were the first to be treated in the newly opened hospital. However, one man with appendicitis could not wait for the surgery unit to be reassembled. A couple of days after his arrival at the internment camp, the Japanese sent him off to an outside hospital to be treated, but he died on the way there.

Eric was in demand both as a teacher and as a member of the athletics department. In the end, he agreed to work a half day for each, which meant that instead of having a three-hour workday like everyone else, he had a six-hour workday.

Teaching was the biggest challenge. The teachers had no chalk or chalkboards, and the children had not much paper and very few pencils. The children would use the same piece of paper over and over, erasing everything they had written on it at the end of the day so they could write on it again the following morning. Eric and the other teachers were particularly concerned about the high school students, many of whom were nearing the age when they would be attending university and had already planned to leave China soon to pursue their education. With few textbooks and no equipment in the camp, it was very difficult for these students to do upper high school work. The teachers tried hard to make up for this lack, but it was difficult to overcome.

One of Eric's students confided in him that her dream was to study chemistry at university in England. Eric made it a priority to do everything he could to help her. He spent evenings sketching and labeling chemistry equipment she would need to do experiments. Then he wrote about how the equipment would be used to conduct the experiments. Even though the young woman never touched a piece of real chemistry equipment in the camp, Eric's sketches were so accurate that she was able to imagine doing the experiments. When she left Weihsien Internment Camp and finally got to take a university acceptance examination, she scored so well she was accepted to study chemistry.

Many of the missionaries in the camp were from the China Inland Mission, founded by English missionary Hudson Taylor in 1865. As it happened, the oldest intern in Weihsien was Hudson Taylor's son Herbert, a snowy-haired man of eighty-three. Herbert Taylor, or Grandpa, as everyone called him, came to the camp with a group of ninety-seven parentless children, most of whom were children of China Inland Mission missionaries and had been at the China Inland Mission boarding school in Chefoo. When the school was captured by the Japanese, all the children there were sent to Weihsien Internment Camp. Some of the children learned that their parents were in other internment camps; others heard the awful news that their parents had been killed in the fighting. Whatever their circumstances, the ninety-seven parentless children needed a lot of extra help and love from the adults in the camp.

"Uncle Eric" soon became one of the children's favorite people. He gave every spare minute of his time to working with the children. He supervised hockey games, and after each game he took the hockey sticks back to his dormitory to repair them for a game the next day. He had found Flo's dining room curtains in one of the trunks under his bed and had torn them into strips, which he wrapped around the hockey sticks to repair them. Eric also ran a Friday night youth group with square dancing, chess tournaments, puppet plays, and quiz shows.

Eric was especially concerned for those who got sick in the camp. Although some of the best surgeons and doctors in all of China were interned in Weihsien, they did not have the medicines and equipment needed to properly treat all their patients. Typhoid, malaria, and dysentery were common ailments. At one point, there were too many sick people to house them all in the hospital, so it was decided that the two patients who had typhoid and were extremely contagious would be housed in the morgue. The two patients were a Catholic nun and a twelve-year-old girl. The girl was one of the parentless children from Chefoo, and Eric could only imagine how frightening it must have been for her to be lying deathly ill in a morgue. In spite of the fact that he might catch typhoid himself, he visited her every afternoon in the morgue. He would cheer her up with stories of what had happened in school that day. Several days after the two patients had been moved to the morgue, the nun died, and young girl remained there alone. Eric's visits gave her the will to live, and eventually she did recover. She was always grateful to Eric for his extra care.

Eric was probably the most popular person in the whole camp. His roommates got tired of the constant stream of children parading past the door looking for Uncle Eric. Finally, one of Eric's roommates made a big sign and hung it outside the door. The sign read, "Eric Liddell is IN/OUT," with either the "In" or the "Out" covered up. This was the only way that Eric's roommates could think of to get some peace!

The most difficult thing about camp life was that it could become very boring. Nothing seemed to change from day to day or week to week. (Eventually, the monotony drove some internees to suffer mental breakdowns.) The food was always a major topic of conversation, though it was the same food day in and day out. Breakfast consisted of two slices of bread, without butter, and a bowl of porridge, without milk. Lunch was nicknamed "S.O.S.," which stood for "Same Old Stew." It was a grayish, globby mixture made from eggplant and chopped-up weeds picked from around the camp. Dinner was the S.O.S. from lunch, with water added to it to make soup. Of course, this didn't fool even the smallest children in the camp, who soon realized they were being fed a repeat of lunch.

Occasionally, the Swiss consul was allowed to visit the camp. He would bring medicine and Red Cross parcels for the prisoners. It was as though everyone in camp had a birthday when Red Cross parcels arrived. Not a crumb of the food in the parcels was wasted, nor were the containers the food came in. The Engineering Department, comprising men who had previously overseen the construction of some of China's finest buildings and bridges, collected all the empty cans and reshaped them into molds to be used to turn coal dust into small bricks that would be used to fire the stoves in the kitchen and the boiler in the hospital.

The Red Cross also arranged for letters to be carried in and out of camp, though the letter writers had to obey very strict rules. Eric, like everyone else, was given a form letter, on which was a space for the name and address of the person writing the letter and the name and address of the person receiving the letter. Underneath was a grid five rows across and five rows down, making twenty-five spaces. In those spaces a prisoner was to write his or her letter. One word per space was strictly enforced, so the writer had to think very carefully before he or she wrote anything down. On the back of the form was another twenty-five space grid for the receiver to send a response. On the average, it took six months for the letter to get to the intended person and another six months for the response to get back to Weihsien.

Even though they were being held against their will, many of those interned in the camp, including Eric, did everything they could think of to make the experience as pleasant as possible. Different people got together and offered over a hundred classes for adults to attend when they were not working. The classes ranged from Latin to ballroom dancing, opera to algebra. (Some classes were a lot more popular than others!) Every weekend there were concerts or plays, and on Sundays there were church services, beginning with the Salvation Army service early in the morning and ending with a Catholic mass in the late afternoon.

The camp also had a thriving black market. Cash and belongings from inside the camp were smuggled out in exchange for eggs and fruit. A group of Roman Catholic Trappist monks were very useful here; their long robes were perfect for hiding things. The leader of the monks was an Australian named Father Scanlan. Night after night, Father Scanlan would collect eggs from a drainage tunnel that ran under the camp's brick walls. Small Chinese boys would crawl into the tunnel and leave the eggs where the monks could reach in and scoop them up and hide them under their robes.

One night, the plan backfired, and Father Scanlan was caught. The entire camp waited and wondered what his punishment would be. Finally, the Japanese called a community meeting, where Father Scanlan's fate would be announced. The Japanese commander of Weihsien Internment Camp announced to everyone that Father Scanlan was to receive a severe punishment for trying to trick the Japanese. He was to spend two weeks in solitary confinement. When it heard this, the crowd broke into wild roars of laughter. Old women laughed until tears rolled down their cheeks, and men slapped each other on the back.

The Japanese led Father Scanlan away, totally bewildered at the reaction of the crowd. What they did not know was that Father Scanlan and his group of Trappist monks, before arriving at the camp, had spent fifteen years without saying a word to anyone. When they joined the order, each monk had taken a vow of silence! Because of the unusual situation they faced being interned, they had been temporarily released from their vow. The monks were used to solitude and silence, and putting Father

Scanlan in solitary confinement for two weeks was not punishment to him at all. It was more like returning him to the way he had lived before being brought to the camp. Father Scanlan's "punishment" was the camp joke for months afterwards. The Japanese, though, never understood why their foreign prisoners had laughed so much when the monk's punishment was announced.

Numerous competitions were held to help cut the monotony as the weeks rolled into months. Rat-catching contests were sponsored by the Medical Department. The record was held by one of the Chefoo teachers and two of his students, who had managed to catch sixty-eight rats in a day. Fly catching was even better. Some of the boys in Eric's Bible study class found that they could catch over fifty of them during one lesson alone. Naturally, there were also many sports competitions, most of which Eric organized. There were cricket and hockey matches, and baseball, courtesy of the American prisoners. The Trappist monks somehow managed to make up the best baseball team and won most of the games.

Eric also organized running contests. Those interned in the camp knew that he held an Olympic Gold Medal in running, and they all loved to watch him run. Towards the end of 1944, though, something happened at one of these running contests that sent a shock wave through Weihsien. It was a crisp autumn day, and Eric was entered in a race. Whenever he ran, he always ran as fast as he could, but on this particular day, Eric lost his race to one of the schoolboys. Word buzzed around the camp. Eric Liddell had lost a race. What could be wrong with him?

Some people thought he was just slowing down as he got older, but his friend Annie Buchan, the matron from the Siao Chang hospital, knew better. She noticed that Eric was not as strong as he had been and was looking very pale. She urged him to cut down on some of his workload. She felt that he was working far too hard, and he probably was. Aside from the responsibilities of teaching and organizing sports that he had been assigned twenty months earlier, he had accepted the responsibility of being warden of Blocks 23 and 24. These blocks housed two hundred thirty single adults and children. The warden's job was to make sure that everyone made it to roll call on time and to keep the peace between people who had been crammed together for far too long to keep their tempers.

At first Eric laughed when Annie told him he was working too hard, but before long, his body seemed to be telling him the same thing. He began to get bad headaches, and even the smell of food made him sick. He would lie for hours on his bed with a wet cloth over his eyes. The children who came to ask Uncle Eric to referee a game of cricket or mend a broken hockey stick yet again were stunned when they were told he was too sick to help them. It sounded impossible. Uncle Eric was always the one helping sick people.

Christmas 1944 came and went, and Eric felt a little better, but he never fully recovered. Then in January, just after his forty-third birthday, he came down with what the doctors thought was a case of the flu, which many other people had at that time. More internees were getting sick than ever before, partly because the tide of the war was turning against the Japanese. As a result, the Japanese were less organized and had less money and resources to keep their foreign prisoners alive and well fed.

By February, most of the internees at Weihsien Internment Camp were malnourished, and the doctors were constantly trying new ideas to get vitamins and minerals, especially for the children. Nothing was wasted. Many of the children had little enamel left on their teeth because of the lack of calcium in their diet. To help with this situation, eggshells were crushed into a powder and spooned into the mouths of unwilling children. Peanut shells were ground up, too, and used as flour to make bread. If this bread was eaten hot, it was digestible, but if it was left to cool, it became as hard as a rock!

In February, Red Cross parcels were delivered to the camp. After devouring the food contained in them, for the first time in weeks, most of the internees felt stronger and were able to work again, but not Eric. The good food seemed to make no difference to him at all. Then, after several weeks in the hospital, Eric had a small stroke. The doctors began to suspect that there was something seriously wrong with him, but they did not have the equipment to diagnose the problem.

After the stroke, Eric started to feel a little better. The doctor gave him permission to get out of bed and go for short walks around the compound. The next day, Eric wrote a letter to Flo. He told her he had been working too hard and the doctors suggested he do something less stressful. In the letter he sent his love to Flo, Patricia, Heather, and Maureen, whom he had not yet seen. Very slowly, he walked to the camp post office and mailed the letter, which was postmarked February 21, 1945.

Later that day, a little girl whose parents were London Missionary Society missionaries came to visit Eric. She sat and chattered to Uncle Eric for a while. Suddenly, Eric began to cough and couldn't stop. The girl got scared and raced into the hallway to find a nurse or doctor. Annie Buchan came running to her old friend's side. She held Eric's hand. Eric looked up at her and said, "Annie, it is surrender." Somehow Annie knew what he meant. Eric was about to die. Soon after, he fell into a coma. At half past nine that night, Eric Liddell "surrendered" and died.

The next morning the camp was covered with a beautiful dusting of snow. As the internees gathered for morning roll call, the news of Eric's death spread throughout the camp. After roll call, many people stood in small groups, too stunned at the news to even go inside out of the cold. For days, the camp mourned.

Eric Liddell's funeral service was held on Saturday, February 24, 1945, three days after his death. A. P. Cullen led the service. Perhaps no one outside of the Liddell family knew Eric as well or for as long as he had. He had been a teacher at Eltham College in London and had known Eric as a ten-year-old schoolboy there. Later in life, the two of them had served together as teachers at the Anglo-Chinese college. They had also shared an apartment after Flo and the girls had left for Canada. Years before, Eric had told A. P. Cullen that he wanted "Be Still My Soul" sung at his funeral. The congregation sang the hymn softly as the schoolchildren formed an honor guard for the pallbearers carrying Eric's coffin to walk through.

About thirty funerals were held in Weihsien Internment Camp. Eric Liddell's was the largest by far. It seemed that everyone had a special reason to remember this exceptional man.

Chapter 17

A Very Special Person

Two months later, Florence Liddell was standing in the kitchen of her parents' home in Toronto, where she was staying. Two family friends knocked at the door, and Flo invited them in. From the expression on their faces, Flo guessed something was wrong. As she dried her hands on a dish towel, she tired to imagine what it could be. She never thought for a single moment that her friends had come to tell her about her husband's death.

As soon as she heard the news, Flo began to shudder. She felt as though something had grabbed her stomach and was squeezing it. As she slumped into a chair, huge sobs began to erupt. Flo wept bitterly, trying to come to terms in her heart and her mind with what she had just heard. How could it be? The last time she had seen Eric he was a strong, healthy thirty-eight-year-old man. Now she had to accept the fact that he'd died in a Japanese internment camp. It hardly seemed possible. Flo's visitors explained that the doctors in Weihsien had performed an autopsy on Eric's body and had found a massive tumor on the left side of Eric's brain. Flo took some comfort in this. As a nurse, she knew that in 1945 there was nothing that could have been done to save Eric's life, not even in the most modern hospital in the world.

"The Flying Scotsman, Dead at 43." These words, printed in large black type, stopped many Scottish men and women in their tracks as they walked past newspaper stands from Edinburgh to Glasgow. The newspapers rushed to outdo each other in praise for their departed national hero.

"Scotland has lost a son who did her proud every hour of his life," reported the *Glasgow Evening News*. "One of the best known and most admired men who ever took part in sport, whose devotion to his principles won him the highest esteem," declared the *Edinburgh Evening News*.

Just as the whole of Weihsien Internment Camp had mourned Eric's death, so, it seemed, did all of Scotland. Memorial services were held in every city and village in the nation.

A national committee was formed to launch the Eric Liddell Memorial Fund. Collections were taken up at rugby games, foot races, school fairs, and church picnics. The money soon mounted up. Many people, both rich and poor, wanted to honor the memory of a man they were proud of. The money from the fund was for two things. First, money was given to Flo to help her raise the three daughters Eric had left behind. Second, a yearly prize was set up in Eric's name: The Eric Liddell Challenge Trophy was awarded to the best performance of the year at the Scottish Schools Athletic Association Championship track meet.

Eltham College in London added an extension to one of its buildings and named it Liddell House.

On August 17, 1945, six months after Eric had been buried, the internees at Weihsien heard an airplane buzzing overhead. The schoolchildren raced outside and were soon joined by the cooks, clothes washers, and everyone else who was not in a hospital bed. The plane turned and swept low over the camp. It was a B-24 bomber, an American plane. The internees went wild with joy. They waved shirts and towels and yelled until they were hoarse. The plane turned again and this time came even closer. They people on the ground could see the pilot waving back to them. They could also read the name painted on the side of the plane: "Armored Angel."

Suddenly the plane veered to the north and climbed steeply, as it if were going to fly off. But then a door on the side of the plane opened, and seven paratroopers jumped out.

The internees could not be stopped. They forgot all about the Japanese guards as they surged towards the massive gates that had held them captive for two years. The Japanese guards stepped back as the gates were pushed open. The prisoners ran towards the paratroopers. Within minutes, they found the GIs and hoisted them onto their shoulders. Amidst cheers and shouts, the GIs were paraded triumphantly back to camp. Everyone knew they were free. It was only a matter of time before they would see their families and their homelands again.

Over the next month, Weihsien Internment Camp was closed down. First the sick and elderly were shipped out, and then unaccompanied children, followed by families and single men and women. As they left, many people made one last trip to the graveyard where a simple wooden cross marked the grave of a man who had been too good of a friend to ever forget.

In the years to come, many of the internees at Weihsien would write books and magazine articles about their experiences. Even though there had been up to eighteen hundred people in the camp, every single written account of life at Weihsien includes memories of Eric Liddell. In *A Boy's War,* David Mitchell tells how Uncle Eric would organize their sports meetings. In *Shantung Compound: The Story of Men and Women Under Pressure,* Gilkey Langdon writes that Eric Liddell was one of the few people in camp everyone trusted to be fair. In another book, *Courtyard of the Happy Way,* Norman Cliff writes of Eric: "The most outstanding Weihsien personality…in his early forties, quiet-spoken and with a permanent smile. Eric was the finest Christian man I have ever had the privilege of meeting."

Finally, the famous British filmmaker Sir David Puttnam heard about the modest Scotsman who had impacted so many lives. He decided to make a movie about Eric which he called *Chariots of Fire.* In 1981, the movie won the Academy Award for best picture.

Eric would probably have laughed if he had known a movie would be made about him. He never considered himself anything special. He was just a man who tried to honor God and help people in need. In the end, achieving those two simple goals made him a very special person to countless people around the world.

Bibliography

Cliff, Norman. *Courtyard of the Happy Way*. Arthur James Ltd., 1977.

Magnusson, Sally. *The Flying Scotsman*. Quartet Books, 1981.

Mitchell, David A. *A Boy's War*. OMF Press, 1988.

Swift, Catherine. *Eric Liddell*. Bethany House Publishers, 1990.

Thomson, D. P. *Scotland's Greatest Athlete*. The Research Unit, Crieff, Perthshire, 1970.

Wilson, Julian. *Complete Surrender*. Monarch, 1996.

About the Authors

Janet and Geoff Benge are a husband and wife writing team with more than thirty years of writing experience. Janet is a former elementary school teacher. Geoff holds a degree in history. Originally from New Zealand, the Benges spent ten years serving with Youth With A Mission. They have two daughters, Laura and Shannon, and an adopted son, Lito. They make their home in the Orlando, Florida, area.

Christian Heroes: Then & Now are available in paperback, e-book, and audiobook formats, with more coming soon!

www.HeroesThenAndNow.com

Also from Janet and Geoff Benge...

More adventure-filled biographies for ages 10 to 100!

Christian Heroes: Then and Now

Gladys Aylward: The Adventure of a Lifetime • 978-1-57658-019-6
Nate Saint: On a Wing and a Prayer • 978-1-57658-017-2
Hudson Taylor: Deep in the Heart of China • 978-1-57658-016-5
Amy Carmichael: Rescuer of Precious Gems • 978-1-57658-018-9
Eric Liddell: Something Greater Than Gold • 978-1-57658-137-7
Corrie ten Boom: Keeper of the Angels' Den • 978-1-57658-136-0
William Carey: Obliged to Go • 978-1-57658-147-6
George Müller: Guardian of Bristol's Orphans • 978-1-57658-145-2
Jim Elliot: One Great Purpose • 978-1-57658-146-9
Mary Slessor: Forward into Calabar • 978-1-57658-148-3
David Livingstone: Africa's Trailblazer • 978-1-57658-153-7
Betty Greene: Wings to Serve • 978-1-57658-152-0
Adoniram Judson: Bound for Burma • 978-1-57658-161-2
Cameron Townsend: Good News in Every Language • 978-1-57658-164-3
Jonathan Goforth: An Open Door in China • 978-1-57658-174-2
Lottie Moon: Giving Her All for China • 978-1-57658-188-9
John Williams: Messenger of Peace • 978-1-57658-256-5
William Booth: Soup, Soap, and Salvation • 978-1-57658-258-9
Rowland Bingham: Into Africa's Interior • 978-1-57658-282-4
Ida Scudder: Healing Bodies, Touching Hearts • 978-1-57658-285-5
Wilfred Grenfell: Fisher of Men • 978-1-57658-292-3
Lillian Trasher: The Greatest Wonder in Egypt • 978-1-57658-305-0
Loren Cunningham: Into All the World • 978-1-57658-199-5
Florence Young: Mission Accomplished • 978-1-57658-313-5
Sundar Singh: Footprints Over the Mountains • 978-1-57658-318-0
C.T. Studd: No Retreat • 978-1-57658-288-6
Rachel Saint: A Star in the Jungle • 978-1-57658-337-1
Brother Andrew: God's Secret Agent • 978-1-57658-355-5
Clarence Jones: Mr. Radio • 978-1-57658-343-2
Count Zinzendorf: Firstfruit • 978-1-57658-262-6
John Wesley: The World His Parish • 978-1-57658-382-1
C. S. Lewis: Master Storyteller • 978-1-57658-385-2
David Bussau: Facing the World Head-on • 978-1-57658-415-6
Jacob DeShazer: Forgive Your Enemies • 978-1-57658-475-0
Isobel Kuhn: On the Roof of the World • 978-1-57658-497-2
Elisabeth Elliot: Joyful Surrender • 978-1-57658-513-9
D. L. Moody: Bringing Souls to Christ • 978-1-57658-552-8
Paul Brand: Helping Hands • 978-1-57658-536-8
Dietrich Bonhoeffer: In the Midst of Wickedness • 978-1-57658-713-3
Francis Asbury: Circuit Rider • 978-1-57658-737-9
Samuel Zwemer: The Burden of Arabia • 978-1-57658-738-6

Klaus-Dieter John: Hope in the Land of the Incas • 978-1-57658-826-2
Mildred Cable: Through the Jade Gate • 978-1-57658-886-4
John Flynn: Into the Never Never • 978-1-57658-898-7
Richard Wurmbrand: Love Your Enemies • 978-1-57658-987-8
Charles Mulli: We Are Family • 978-1-57658-894-9
John Newton: Change of Heart • 978-1-57658-909-0
Helen Roseveare: Mama Luka • 978-1-57658-910-6
Norman Grubb: Mission Builder • 978-1-57658-915-1
Albert Schweitzer • 978-1-57658-961-8

Heroes of History

George Washington Carver: From Slave to Scientist • 978-1-883002-78-7
Abraham Lincoln: A New Birth of Freedom • 978-1-883002-79-4
Meriwether Lewis: Off the Edge of the Map • 978-1-883002-80-0
George Washington: True Patriot • 978-1-883002-81-7
William Penn: Liberty and Justice for All • 978-1-883002-82-4
Harriet Tubman: Freedombound • 978-1-883002-90-9
John Adams: Independence Forever • 978-1-883002-50-3
Clara Barton: Courage under Fire • 978-1-883002-51-0
Daniel Boone: Frontiersman • 978-1-932096-09-5
Theodore Roosevelt: An American Original • 978-1-932096-10-1
Douglas MacArthur: What Greater Honor • 978-1-932096-15-6
Benjamin Franklin: Live Wire • 978-1-932096-14-9
Christopher Columbus: Across the Ocean Sea • 978-1-932096-23-1
Laura Ingalls Wilder: A Storybook Life • 978-1-932096-32-3
Orville Wright: The Flyer • 978-1-932096-34-7
Captain John Smith: A Foothold in the New World • 978-1-932096-36-1
Thomas Edison: Inspiration and Hard Work • 978-1-932096-37-8
Alan Shepard: Higher and Faster • 978-1-932096-41-5
Ronald Reagan: Destiny at His Side • 978-1-932096-65-1
Davy Crockett: Ever Westward • 978-1-932096-67-5
Milton Hershey: More Than Chocolate • 978-1-932096-82-8
Billy Graham: America's Pastor • 978-1-62486-024-9
Ben Carson: A Chance at Life • 978-1-62486-034-8
Louis Zamperini: Redemption • 978-1-62486-049-2
Elizabeth Fry: Angel of Newgate • 978-1-62486-064-5
William Wilberforce: Take Up the Fight • 978-1-62486-057-7
William Bradford: Plymouth's Rock • 978-1-62486-092-8
Ernest Shackleton: Going South • 978-1-62486-093-5
Benjamin Rush: The Common Good • 978-1-62486-123-9
Dwight Eisenhower: Supreme Commander • 978-1-62486-142-0
Frederick Douglass: The Right to Dignity • 978-1-62486-151-2
Winston Chruchill: Resolute • 978-1-62486-153-6

Available in paperback, e-book, and audiobook formats.
Unit Study Curriculum Guides are available for many biographies.
www.YWAMpublishing.com or www.Heroesofhistory.com